OUT of the SHADOWS

Author Biographies

Anne Marie West was born to Fred West and Catherine Costello in 1964. She now lives in Gloucester with her two children.

Virginia Hill has been a journalist with the *Daily Star* for eleven years. Born in Cardiff she now lives in Wiltshire.

OUT of the SHADOWS

ANNE MARIE WEST
With Virginia Hill

SIMON & SCHUSTER
LONDON · SYDNEY · NEW YORK · TOKYO · SINGAPORE · TORONTO

First published in Great Britain by Simon & Schuster, 1995
A Viacom Company

Copyright © Express Newspapers PLC, 1995

This book is copyright under the Berne Convention
No reproduction without permission
All rights reserved

The right of Express Newspapers PLC and Virginia Hill to
be identified as authors of this work has been asserted in
accordance with sections 77 and 78 of the Copyright, Designs and
Patents Act 1988

Simon & Schuster Ltd
West Garden Place
Kendal Street
London W2 2AQ

Simon & Schuster of Australia Pty Ltd
Sydney

A CIP catalogue record for this book is available
from the British Library

ISBN 0-671-51191-2

Typeset in Goudy Modern 13/15pt by
Palimpsest Book Production Limited, Polmont, Stirlingshire
Printed and bound in Great Britain by
Butler & Tanner, Frome & London

For 'my girls' – Caz and Chell, and in loving memory of my mother Catherine and sisters Charmaine and Heather.

There is nothing more precious in the world than the feeling of being wanted.

Contents

Chronology of events	1
1 The Nightmare Begins	5
2 My Sister Heather	17
3 My Mother's Family	25
4 My Father's Family	33
5 The Day I Met Rose	45
6 My Sister Charmaine	55
7 Raped By My Father	67
8 Family Life	73
9 Fred West	83
10 Rose West	93
11 My School Years	105
12 Phil	119
13 On the Run	131
14 Marriage	145
15 Phil	163
16 Why?	173
17 The Ones That Got Away	179
18 The Day My Father Died	195
19 Funerals	205
20 Life Now	217
21 The Trial	229
22 The Verdict	237
The Victims	241

Acknowledgements

Thanks go to Martin Stote and Dave Newman of the *Daily Star* for their contributions, help, constant support and friendship during the preparation of this book; also to former *Daily Star* editor Brian Hitchen, editor Phil Walker, news editor Hugh Whittow and former night news editor Tom Hendry.

Heartfelt appreciation to Jim and Lyn Hill for their encouragement and help with the manuscript; to Ken Goodwin of Central Television for his support, to Sue Bailey and Mark Burgess of Express Newspapers Books Department, the Express legal team, and Martin Fletcher of Simon & Schuster for their help and advice.

Anne Marie West and Virginia Hill

Chronology of Events

29 September 1941: Frederick Walter Stephen West born, in the tiny farming hamlet of Much Marcle, the eldest child of farmhand Walter West and his wife Daisy, a housemaid.

17 November 1962: Fred marries café waitress Catherine 'Rena' Costello, who has been living in nearby Ledbury but hails from Glasgow.

April – May 1967: Anne McFall, aged eighteen, from Glasgow, vanishes. A friend of Catherine Costello she had been working for the West family as a nanny. She was eight months' pregnant when she disappeared.

March – December 1970: Catherine Costello goes missing.

Spring 1970: Fred West meets fifteen-year-old Rosemary Letts and begins a relationship with her, against the wishes of her parents.

March 1971: Charmaine West, Catherine Costello's daughter by another man, disappears from 25 Midland Road, Gloucester, where she had been living with Fred and Rose.

29 January 1972: Fred and Rose marry at Gloucester Register Office.

6 December 1972: Teenager Caroline Owens is kidnapped and subjected to a horrifying sex ordeal by Fred and Rose West. She had previously worked as their nanny.

12 January 1973: Fred and Rose appear at Gloucester Magistrates Court, charged with assault, causing actual bodily harm and indecent assault against Caroline Owens. They plead guilty and are fined £50 each.

April 1973: Lynda Gough, aged nineteen, disappears. She had been living in a flat at the Wests' home, 25 Cromwell Street. Rose tells her mother that Lynda has moved to Weston-super-Mare.

November 1973: Carol Ann Cooper, aged fifteen, goes missing from a local children's home.

27 December 1973: Student Lucy Partington, twenty-one, fails to return after visiting a friend in Cheltenham.

16 April 1974: Twenty-one-year-old Swiss student Therese Siegenthaler sets off to hitch-hike from London to Holyhead for a planned trip to Ireland. She never arrives.

15 November 1974: Shirley Hubbard, aged fifteen, goes missing on her way to work at Debenhams in Worcester.

11 April 1975: Juanita Mott, seventeen, does not come home after a night out. She had previously lived at 25 Cromwell Street.

Out of the Shadows

9 May 1978: Shirley Robinson, a lodger living with the Wests at 25 Cromwell Street, vanishes. Nineteen-year-old Shirley was eight months' pregnant with Fred's child at the time.

September 1979: Alison Chambers, aged seventeen, fails to turn up for her work experience job and is never seen again. She had been a regular visitor to 25 Cromwell Street.

June 1987: Heather West, the eldest daughter of Fred and Rose, disappears. The couple claim she has run away from home with a lesbian.

June 1993: Fred and Rose West walk free from Gloucester Crown Court after sex charges involving one of their children are dropped. No one in the family is prepared to give evidence against them.

25 February 1994: Fred and Rose are arrested by police in connection with the disappearance of their daughter Heather. Fred is held but Rose is released on bail.

26 February 1994: Heather's body is found in the garden of 25 Cromwell Street. Fred is charged with her murder.

28 February 1994: The body of Alison Chambers is discovered in the garden. Four hours later, Shirley Robinson is uncovered.

March 1994: Police begin to search the cellar at 25 Cromwell Street. Five more bodies are found over the next few days. Lynda Gough is then discovered under the bathroom.

10 April 1994: The body of Catherine Costello is found in Letterbox Field, Much Marcle.

20 April 1994: Rose West is re-arrested by detectives.

25 April 1994: Rose West is charged with the murder of Lynda Gough.

4 May 1994: Charmaine West's body is discovered at 25 Midland Road, the family's former home.

6 May 1994: Rose is jointly charged with her husband on five counts of murder.

7 June 1994: After a hole the size of a swimming pool is dug in Fingerpost Field in Much Marcle the body of Anne McFall is disinterred.

1 January 1995: Fred West hangs himself while on remand at Winson Green Prison, Birmingham.

14 February 1995: Rose West is committed for trial on ten murder charges following a seven-day hearing at Dursley Magistrates Court.

October 1995: The trial of Rose West begins at Winchester Crown Court.

I

The Nightmare Begins

The doorbell rang at almost the same time as the telephone. I didn't know which to answer first. The phone was in the hallway, so I grabbed that, wondering why I was in such demand at eight o'clock in the morning. My stepmother's voice exploded in my ear. Her words sent a chill to my heart, even though I could not comprehend their meaning at that moment. I clutched at the receiver, my hand shaking.

'If you think anything of me or your dad, especially your dad, you'll say nothing and keep your mouth shut.'

There was no preamble, no greeting, she slammed the phone down, leaving me with the dialling tone. I dithered, but only for a second, because the doorbell buzzed again, insistently. Smoothing down my hair, I opened the door. The woman standing before me was dressed in plain clothes, but I knew enough people in Gloucester to recognise her as WDC Hazel Savage. It wasn't hard to work out that the smartly dressed man beside her was a detective too.

Hazel looked me in the eye in the very direct manner which I later came to realise was her trademark. In her late forties, with around thirty years' experience in the force, her very appearance spelled out no nonsense. Her short hair was brushed back from her narrow face; her dark skirt suit as straight and to the point as she was. 'I expect you know who we are. I suppose you've been warned we would be coming,' she said.

'Yes, I know who you are,' I replied simply. 'Come in.'

Now the telephone call made sense; the visit a week earlier from my younger sister Mae fell into place. At last someone was going to investigate my father and my stepmother, finally maybe their bizarre sexual crimes and years of abuse of me would finally be revealed. Yet I didn't know then, and could never have imagined, how much more was to be uncovered. I knew I was the daughter of a child-abuser who had married a sadistic and violent woman with an insatiable appetite for sex. It was another two years before I discovered that I was the daughter of a serial killer and the stepdaughter of a woman capable of evil beyond my worst nightmares.

Let me say from the outset that I never knew about the bodies. That may be hard to believe, but I was only fifteen when I ran away from our home in Cromwell Street and still a child. I knew only my own torment, my own suffering and my desperate need to escape. More than fifteen years later, I can only suppose that some basic survival instinct made me act. But back then I knew only that I had to get away. There can be little doubt that if I hadn't escaped when I did they would have been bringing out my body from the cellar as well.

Out of the Shadows

A week before Hazel Savage and her colleague came to call, my younger half-sister Mae had appeared on my doorstep. I was surprised at the unexpected visit. She is eight years younger than I am and the circumstances of our upbringing meant we had not been close in recent years. I automatically made us both a cup of tea, unaware of the bombshell she was about to drop. I sat down shakily on the dark brown sofa in my living room when Mae told me why she had come. She was very matter-of-fact about it, and had no idea what horrors her news brought flooding back to me.

Another daughter in the family had told Mae that our father, Fred West, had raped a fourteen-year-old girl we knew. A court order and my own desire to protect her prevents me from naming her. As if the appalling sex act were not enough, a video had been made of the attack. Mae, knowing of my experiences at the hands of our father, had come to me for help. I felt numb and sick at the thought that someone else was having to suffer in the same way I had. It was something I had feared for a long time, but I had closed my mind against it by telling myself that there must have been a reason for my suffering and that by accepting it I had in some way prevented the others from being harmed. Now I had to face the fact that another young girl was being made to relive my nightmare. Once the shock receded, I was determined to put a stop to it.

I asked Mae to try to get her hands on the video as evidence. I would then deal with the rest. I don't know quite what I planned to do — go to the authorities in some form, I suppose. I had been brought up not to trust the police, the welfare, the medical profession, or any other person in authority. We were brainwashed into believing they would only do us harm. But even so, I knew I had to go to someone.

Mae agreed to try to get hold of the evidence. We both knew it would not be possible for me to do so. I was not a welcome guest at 25 Cromwell Street. If I wanted to visit I had to make an appointment. Turning up now would only alert Fred and Rose.

I never knew whether Mae found the video. She promised to get in touch within a few days but I heard nothing from her for the rest of that week. I called the charity Childline for advice but was told that the victim would have to make contact with them personally. I didn't know which way to turn. In the end I decided to hold fire until Mae contacted me again.

As it turned out, things came to a head without my intervention. The fourteen-year-old had bravely confided in a schoolfriend and an anonymous call had been made to the police. They sent two officers to Cromwell Street on the pretext of investigating a case of stolen goods and handling. It would not be the first time the law had called on Fred to discuss such matters, but this time they got an unusual reaction to their apparently innocent inquiries. Rose immediately sent all the children to their bedrooms (there would have been five of them, aged between nine and sixteen, living at home at the time). With the youngsters out of the way and therefore safe from questioning, she lost her rag and raged at the officers until they had no choice but to arrest her. My stepmother's bizarre behaviour aroused their suspicions and the social services were called in to look after the younger children while she was quizzed at the police station.

It was the beginning of the case against my father and Rose. It was the first concrete clue that things were not right at number 25 Cromwell Street and hadn't been for a long time. The first step on the road to discovering what had happened to so many people who had vanished mysteriously from my life: my real mother, my sister Charmaine, my sister Heather, my friend Shirley, and the daughters of many other anxious parents who had waited and wondered for years.

Fred and Rose later walked away from the charges brought against them concerning the fourteen-year-old. They thought they would keep walking, but the case had triggered deep suspicions in the minds of Hazel Savage and her colleagues and the path they eventually took led my father to meet his maker and Rose her judge and jury. Once the police had talked to Rose about her involvement in the assault on the girl, they took Dad in for questioning. Of course, they both denied the charges, and no one ever found the video, but two teenage girls were asked to give statements.

The fourteen-year-old told the police what had happened to her and the sixteen-year-old described what she had witnessed. She claimed she had seen our father lead the younger girl into Rose's private bedroom. She heard screaming and when the girl emerged from the room she was crying and there was blood on her legs. Rose's reaction when the fourteen-year-old girl had tried to talk to her about it had apparently been: 'Oh well, you were asking for it.'

There was only one way to back up these girls' statements, and that was to make one of my own. I hadn't been there to see what had happened to her, but I could tell the police that the same thing had happened before — to me. I was appalled by what Hazel Savage told me that terrible morning and when she asked me to go with them and make a statement I had no hesitation, although I knew it would be hard. The detectives took me to Tuffley Police Station, about two miles away, in an unmarked car.

The station itself is not intimidating. It is in Upper

Tuffley, on a long winding hill lined with smart houses, a large off-white building which looks like two 1950s council houses joined together. Hazel took me to a room upstairs sparsely furnished with just a desk and a few high-backed chairs. The policemen downstairs cast us curious glances as we passed through.

In those days I smoked, and Hazel kept giving me cigarettes and cups of tea to calm my nerves. She knew I wouldn't want to say a lot; she understood my background and could tell how difficult the situation was for me. But I was hurting for that girl. She was being made to look a liar and they were doing what they had done to me. I thought, 'No, I can't let this happen.' I had gone through my whole life being called a liar and a wicked child. I knew the girl wasn't lying, and I wasn't going to allow them to say she was.

It took all day and much heartache, but I made my statement. I told Hazel Savage things I had never told anyone. I tried to do it calmly and quietly, and I tried not to watch her reaction. I was ashamed of what I was having to tell her. I had lived for so long with the belief that everything that had happened to me was my own fault, but now, as I talked about it for the first time ever, at the age of twenty-eight and with two children of my own, it began to dawn on me that no child could be to blame for the actions of two such sick people.

I told Hazel how my father had raped me when I was just eight years old and how Rose had helped him. I told her, too, about a bizarre assault when I was twelve, when my father and Rose were experimenting with artificial insemination. Yet I left so much out. I felt uncomfortable about a lot of it because it sounded so unbelievable, and besides, there were some things I couldn't imagine ever talking to anybody about. So the statement I made was truthful but selective. I recounted only what I thought might help the girl. To have told everything would have taken weeks — which in fact it did, two years later, when Dad was charged with murder.

But there was one other thing I mentioned to Hazel in the hope that she might be able to help me. I told her about my missing sister Heather, and how I had looked for her since the day she vanished. I had travelled the West Country in search of her and had even contacted the Samaritans. Perhaps, I suggested, the police, with all their powers, could do more. Hazel said she would do her best and promised to let me know if she ever found a trace of Heather. It was another two years before she was able to keep that promise.

I went through hell making that statement to Hazel. It brought back horrors I thought I had blocked out forever. It shook me to the core and left me traumatised, despite the façade I maintained for the sake of my own two girls. Having suffered in making it I suffered even more after I withdrew it, but I felt I had no choice. I will have to live for the rest of my life with the knowledge that I took back everything I said a matter of weeks afterwards. But to this day, although in some ways I feel ashamed and so dreadfully sorry for letting down those girls, I can't think there was any other way.

I knew all my siblings were safe and in the care of the social services. I knew Dad couldn't get at them and that Rose would never be allowed to have them back. But I knew who Fred and Rose could get at — me and my two children. And I knew they wouldn't hesitate to do it.

I can't remember the actual date I withdrew the statement, but it must have been a couple of months after I made it. I was so worried about my own family, but no one would take me seriously. I asked the police for protection, but they couldn't understand why I thought I needed it. Everyone seemed to think I was making a fuss over nothing, but I was terrified. Given what has come to light now, I had every reason to be. But then all I could think of was Rose's temper, the way she would catch you by the throat in a split-second or take a knife to you. She was not a person to upset lightly and she, as a co-accused, would see my statement.

My fear took over. I think I started to go back and open some of the doors I had locked over the years and found myself realising that this clouded dream was in fact the reality of my childhood. Now I had talked about it, it began to come back. It was confusing. I remembered the vicious hidings which often left me so bruised I couldn't go to school, and the abuse and the men and . . . I didn't want to remember any more.

So I retracted my statement, saying it was all a figment of my imagination. I claimed I had lied because I didn't like Fred and Rose. I made myself out to be the liar they had always labelled me. Hazel Savage came and sat on my settee and looked at me for a long time. She had my statement with her. She said: 'Tell me to my face this isn't true.'

I looked at her for a moment and then turned my head away so that she couldn't see my eyes. I told her: 'It's not true. I just made it up.'

Hazel shook her head. 'No. This happened. I know this happened.'

But I would say no more and stood my ground. Hazel cautioned me and told me I could be taken to court for wasting police time and making a false statement, I would be hearing from them about it. Of course, I never did. I told her simply I was frightened of Rose and no one was taking me seriously. I had to think of my own children. We left it at that.

Hazel kept in touch over the next two years with very occasional visits, updating me on her search for my sister Heather. I didn't see her often because there wasn't much to tell. Like me, she had drawn a blank everywhere she looked.

Fred and Rose were cleared in June 1993 of sexually assaulting the girl. No one would give evidence in court. The police didn't bother to tell me what had happened — I read about it in the local paper. The headline was: COUPLE'S DELIGHT AS SEX CASE IS DROPPED. The report described how they had hugged each other in the dock when they realised no evidence was to be offered. My father had faced three charges of raping a fourteen-year-old girl and one of buggery. Rose had been accused of encouraging her husband to have sex with the girl. My heart sank and my guilt increased, but at least their children were still safely in care.

A few months after that court case, Hazel Savage was back on my doorstep. She wanted to know about a family joke often repeated by the children to their foster parents. The carers thought the children were genuinely scared of their mother and father and said they frequently expressed a wish not to end up like their big sister Heather — under the patio in the back garden. It was something I too had mentioned to Hazel, and it was beginning to make her suspicious. I explained how it had become my father's little jest and told of the first time I had heard it.

A number of us had been sitting round the kitchen table at 25 Cromwell Street. Dad came out with this line and started to laugh, really laugh. I can remember looking at him and thinking, how strange, you don't laugh at things like that. I was a bit concerned because I had been searching for Heather for so long, but I dismissed my discomfort. It was just a joke, wasn't it?

Hazel obviously didn't think so. She came back some months later, in February 1994, and asked me if I was still concerned about Heather and whether I wanted the search to continue. I did, but I didn't quite take in what she said next.

The day Hazel chose to tell me that the police were going to dig up the garden at Cromwell Street was my younger daughter's seventh birthday. Hazel and her colleague once again called first thing in the morning as I battled to get the children off to school. I can only think that my mind was elsewhere, because it did not really strike me at the time that they meant they were going to be looking for Heather in the garden. Somehow I gained the impression they were simply going to take a look around the house for clues, arrest Dad and question him about what might have happened to Heather.

The next day, a Friday, the tenacious detective was back again. She said that Dad had been taken in for questioning and was in the cells. She revealed little beyond the fact that Dad was helping them their with inquiries.

I learned the truth on the Saturday afternoon in a telephone call from another policewoman. Her timing was appalling. My little girl's birthday party was in full swing. I was surrounded by fifteen excited, giggling seven-year-olds. My daughter's teacher was the guest of honour and one or two neighbours were helping out. In the middle of all this I was told that Heather's body had been dug up from the garden of the home we once shared. My father was the chief suspect.

Out of the Shadows

I was shaking. I wanted to cry. I wanted to dissolve into my grief, but I couldn't. Instead I hunted through the kitchen cupboards and found a bottle of sherry left over from Christmas and poured some into a tumbler. It was sweet and dark and I hoped it would pass for Coca-Cola in front of the children. I made one phone call to my boyfriend, the father of my youngest child, and asked him leave work as soon as possible and come to my house. Then I pinned a smile on my face, took a gulp of sherry and organised another party game. The only children to guess something was wrong were my own, but now was not the time to tell them what was making their mother unhappy.

I was simply stunned. I remember the officer asking me, 'Are you all right? Is there anybody with you?'

I told her: 'I'm doing my daughter's birthday party. I'm fine, fine,' and I rang off.

The day they dug up my sister's remains they dug up another body too. But they didn't tell me that. I saw it on the local television news.

It was the beginning of my addiction to every news broadcast and newspaper I could find. That was how I obtained my information, along with the rest of the fascinated public. Occasional visits from the police brought nothing. They weren't offering information; they wanted it from me. So it was from the television that I learned, on the day my mother, Catherine Costello, would have been fifty years old, that they had found her body too. It was a newscaster who informed me that the mother I thought had abandoned me as a child had been discovered buried in a field in Much Marcle, my father's home village.

2

My Sister Heather

I searched for years for Heather and never gave up hope of finding her until the police did it for me. They discovered her remains in the garden of the home where we had both grown up. It brought to an end my dream of a happier life for the bright-eyed toddler I had watched grow into a difficult, despondent teenager. We were only half-sisters, but she was the first of the babies in the family I was delegated to look after and I loved her unreservedly. She was a delight; always smiling and cheerful. I remember she had a sort of baby-walker in which she used to scoot around the house. She was never any trouble. I was never jealous of her, despite the favouritism she was shown by Fred and Rose. In fact I was never jealous of any of the other children — I cared too much about them for that.

From the very beginning it seemed that Heather was special to her parents. They used to call her their love-child and often talked about how they had fought the authorities and Rose's parents in order to keep her. Rose had been very young when Heather was born, still only a teenager herself, and no one had approved of her relationship with my father. Yet for parents who claimed she was dear to them, they showed little concern when she disappeared at the age of sixteen. They came up with various stories about the day she left and for years afterwards Fred would claim to have bumped into Heather somewhere or to have received a chatty telephone call from her saying she was fine and working in another part of the country. I followed up some of these leads, travelling as far afield as Torquay in Devon after my father said that Heather was working in a holiday camp there. But no one had ever seen her or even heard of her, and I went home anxious and disheartened each time.

I remember very clearly the last time I saw Heather: I even recall what she was wearing. She had on a baggy white T-shirt and leggings. Her dark brown hair was very long and worn loose. I had made a note in my diary which later helped the police pinpoint exactly when she went missing. The date was 17 June 1987 — my elder daughter Michelle's third birthday. I had a party for her at my home in Gloucester. The family turned out in force, which was, I suppose, quite unusual. Fred and Rose came with all their other children and a few of the neighbours' children gathered for the occasion too. It was a lovely summer's day and I encouraged all the younger ones to go and play in the garden while I got the party tea ready. It was the usual kids' treats — jelly and little cakes and all that sort of thing. I have always enjoyed making special food for the children, probably because that sort of party is a thing I missed out on as a kid.

Heather went out into the garden too but she didn't join in with the younger children, not even her sisters. She spent

Out of the Shadows

most of the afternoon at the far end of the lawn by the shed and wouldn't socialise. I watched her from the kitchen window. She wasn't talking to anyone and mostly kept her back turned to everyone else. Each time I tried to approach Heather and talk to her, my stepmother or my father would be there in an instant. Even when I was looking at her out of the kitchen window Rose came in. It was as if they didn't want me to be alone with Heather. I didn't make too much of it because they never wanted anyone to spend time with any of the kids if they weren't present, but even so I thought it was a little odd. In the end I became concerned enough to send my then husband Chris out to talk to Heather in the garden. She said very little to him and certainly didn't confide what was bothering her. She just stayed where she was at the bottom of the garden, looking so sad. I love taking photographs of my children and I tried to include Heather in the family group shots but she wouldn't co-operate. Instead, in the last picture I have of her, her back is turned defiantly towards the camera.

I really regret that I never got to talk to her that day. We just said hi and goodbye, and that was it. I never got another opportunity. Two days later, I had a telephone call from my father telling me that Heather had left home. He said she was heading for Torquay with a girlfriend and that they were going to try to get work at a holiday camp there. He described the other girl as a 'lemon' — his term for a lesbian — and intimated that he thought Heather was one too. I questioned my father regularly about Heather but he stuck to his story and elaborated on it as time went on. He said Heather and her pal had left together in a white Mini; he said he had caught her sneaking out of the house with her belongings and that he had instructed Rose to give her £100 to keep her going.

Over the following few months he claimed to have both seen and spoken to Heather. He said she had fallen out with her friend and had found a job at a community centre in Gloucestershire. Once again I checked out what he'd told me, to no avail. Fred said that she must have chucked in the job and moved on again. My sister Mae recalls that only a few days after Heather left, a large number of full black refuse bags were put out for the dustman. Now we both realise that they must have contained the belongings that Fred and Rose told us Heather had taken with her.

Heather, as I said, was a lovely baby and a super toddler, but over the years she changed into an angry young woman. I was not at home during those years but I now believe that she must have rebelled against the appalling lifestyle at Cromwell Street and that she was killed for it. I had always cherished the hope that she had escaped the torment I experienced as a child and a teenager, but now it seems that she must have gone through a similar ordeal herself.

Many people would have described Heather as a happy-go-lucky type. I think she tried to put on a brave face for the outside world, but at home she was sad, sometimes aggressive and always angry. She made it clear to Rose she did not approve of what was going on. She was younger than me; she had grown up in a more aware society and she knew that her family life was not normal. She was deeply ashamed of it, but the ever-present violence prevented her from doing anything about it.

Heather was not particularly attractive as she grew older – a bit of a plain Jane, really – but she was a good girl. When she became a teenager Fred began to tease her, and I think that was the beginning of her slide into misery. He would make personal remarks to all of the girls in the family. One of his favourite comments was that we needed a good man to sort us out. I suppose the underlying threat was always that he was the man to do it. In fact, sometimes he would actually say he would do it himself, and he'd turn to one of the younger girls and tell her, 'It will be your turn next.' Another of Fred's homespun philosophies included the line: 'Women are sitting on a goldmine, and if you don't lose your virginity young, then the older you get the more it will send you mental.' This kind of taunt had little effect on me after what I had already been through, but Heather found it harder to deal with. She was a lot more open with her mouth than I had ever been and got away with arguing a lot more.

I don't know why Heather never told me what was happening to her at home. Perhaps she knew I had suffered in the same way, or perhaps she thought I knew and just wasn't prepared to help. But it is too late now to wish she had turned to me so that I could have done something, but 'if only' are two of the saddest words I know. Now that she has gone and so many people have given statements to the police and spoken to journalists I know much more about how she suffered than I did then. I was struggling to make something of my own life away from Cromwell Street, dealing with a violent husband and trying to bring up my own family. It was difficult to be there for all my siblings too.

Heather went to Hucclecote Secondary School from the age of eleven, moving up from St Paul's New Street, just as I had. At secondary school she had a very close friend called Denise Harrison, who has been able to fill in a lot of the gaps in my sister's life and has revealed frightening parallels with my own upbringing. She has given an insight, too, into the last few weeks of Heather's life and into what might have led Fred and Rose to believe it was too risky to let her live.

The danger period began at the time Heather was sitting her GCSE exams just before leaving school for good. She had always said she wanted to be a secretary or to work with animals. She was a bright girl and good at her schoolwork. She passed eight GCSEs but didn't live to see the results.

There were about three or four weeks of the school year left when Denise noticed that Heather was even more morose than normal. Denise later told a newspaper reporter that she found her friend sitting on a wall near Cromwell Street, crying. Heather confided that she had discovered that her mother, Rose, had been having a long affair with the father of another girl she knew. The man, a West Indian, was the father of three of her siblings and she had never known it. Fred and Rose had always explained away their three half-caste children by claiming that they were throwbacks to Fred's gypsy past. It sounds unlikely now, but people, particularly disturbed children, will believe what they want to believe. Heather was desperately upset, and had challenged the man's daughter. The young girl went straight home and told her mother. The father turned up at Cromwell Street the very next day for a showdown. Rose and Fred were furious that Heather had been discussing their business outside the family and she suffered a tremendous beating.

She also revealed to Denise that Fred had been sexually abusing her and that her mother had refused to do anything about it. Like the rest of us, she was too frightened to go to the police or to anybody else. Denise never doubted her friend's story. She had regularly noticed the severe bruising on Heather's arms and legs. She told of how Heather, just as I had done, always refused to shower after sport at school, wore long-sleeved blouses and pulled her socks up way over her knees so that the bruises wouldn't show.

Denise told her own mother all this but her Godfearing family had known Fred socially for years and couldn't believe it of him. Again, if only . . . Heather tried to cry for help but there was no one there to answer.

Who knows exactly what happened in the last few days of her life? I suspect that she intended to get help and maybe even threatened to expose the sleaze of 25 Cromwell Street. I don't believe she knew about the bodies any more than the rest of us; if she had, she would have tried to escape sooner. Denise thinks Fred and Rose could not have killed Heather while she was still at school because she would have been missed. The timing of her death speaks for itself — the date on the murder charge was eight days after she left Hucclecote Secondary. It is ironic that Heather was probably killed because she threatened to tell, for in a way she did reveal the truth anyway: it was the discovery of her body that gave the police more information than she could ever have done when she was alive.

Heather's body was found by the police digging in the back garden of the home we had shared. The remains were jumbled up, with arms, legs, trunk and skull located at different levels. Heather had been decapitated and the body dismembered at the hips using chopping blows with some form of heavy implement. Black plastic bin liners were found around the trunk.

The police didn't believe any more than I did that Heather knew about the bodies buried at Cromwell Street, but closer examination by detectives revealed that Dad and Rose had told a variety of stories to different people who had inquired about my sister. Anne Knight, a friend of my stepmother's, told the police that Rose had said her daughter had left home following 'a hell of a row'. The argument had been over Heather's relationship with a Welsh lesbian and the teenager had gone off with her new friend. Ronald Harrison, the father of Heather's pal Denise, had asked Fred about Heather and was told that she had been assaulting the younger children of the family when she babysat. Rose had given the girl a good hiding and she had left home. Another woman and her daughter had been given the explanation that Rose and Fred had gone out shopping and come home to find Heather gone. To the window-cleaner, a Mr Marshall, they said that Heather had run away from home and assured him that the police had been informed.

It was all a pack of lies. They knew where she was and they regularly held family barbecues over the spot where they had hidden her. It upsets me so much to think of that, and to remember that not one of her possessions was ever found, not a single one. I have nothing left of the sister I loved and helped to bring up except for a few blurred photographs.

I went to 25 Cromwell Street after they found Heather's body and placed some flowers at the gates. I left a short message with them. I was to do the same for my mother and big sister Charmaine. My goodbye to Heather read: 'To my sister Heather, I've searched and sought, I've wept and prayed we'd meet again some sunny day. Missing you so very much. Will always love and remember you. All my fondest love, Big Sis, Anna-Marie.'

3

My Mother's Family

I never really knew much about my family background. It is only now, since all this happened, that I have begun to realise I have uncles, aunts and cousins on my mother's side. It was not something that was ever discussed during my childhood, and it didn't take me long to work out that you didn't ask questions. And in any case, once my father had met Rose, my mother was rarely referred to again. In fact I was under strict instructions never to mention her name in case it 'upset' my new stepmother.

Yet I like to think there was a time when I belonged to a normal family. I can't remember much about it, and maybe to an extent it is my own little fantasy, but I do remember being shown ordinary affection by my father. In my mind's eye I can see him hugging me, telling me I was Dad's girl and that he loved me. And when my real mother vanished he used to say: 'You're all right. You've got your dad. Your dad loves you.' As a small child, I worshipped him – he was everything to me. In the early days he was never cruel or violent. He truly seemed to care. We were a team, me and Dad. I was his little girl and he was my handsome dad. I used to say: 'When I grow up, Dad, I'm going to marry you.' He would ruffle my hair and laugh. It seemed so normal then. Now I look back and wonder if there was something sinister in everything he said or did, even in those days. Against all the odds, deep down I can't help holding on to the thought that in the early years we were a proper family.

When I was four or five Dad used to tell me stories about how he had looked after me when I was a tiny baby. I loved to listen to it all. It was special; it meant he really loved me and had done since the day I was born. When I was about a year old Dad worked as an ice-cream man. He used to drive a van selling cornets and tubs of soft ice-cream in the poor districts of Glasgow. He made me a little cot out of a wooden box and put it under the counter. He took me everywhere with him, and apparently I used to sleep for most of the day with the cheerful tune of the ice-cream van as my lullaby. For years I loved being told that story and picturing myself as a baby with my proud dad serving ice-creams and gazing at me asleep on a shelf under the counter.

I was Christened Anna-Marie but I have since changed the 'a' for an 'e' and call myself simply Anne. It's my way of forging a new identity and blotting out my early years.

I was born in Glasgow, which makes me a Scot although I speak with a bit of a Gloucester accent now. As a young child, however, I was a wee Scots lassie with an accent which could be deciphered only by folk brought up within a few miles' radius of the district in which we lived. In fact it was so bad that when I moved to Gloucester as an infant and spent some time in a children's home because my Dad could not cope alone they had to give me elocution lessons because no one could understand a word I said. That got rid of most of my accent, but even now I still use words and expressions best known north of the border and I am proud to describe myself as Scottish. Friends tell me I pronounce certain words with a Scots lilt occasionally, so the children's home can't have cured it completely.

My mother, Catherine Costello, came from a rough area of Glasgow. She was by all accounts a bit of a bad girl. I don't think she was a nasty person, more of a lovable rogue, from what I can gather. She certainly got herself into some scrapes as a youngster and had just been released from some sort of remand home or detention centre when she met my dad. She would have been about eighteen then. Mum had gained a reputation for being a bit fast and she was undoubtedly one for the men. Growing up in such a tough area, she had learned how to take care of herself. I think deep down she wanted to make something of herself and escape from the life she was leading. Perhaps she thought Dad was her way out. From what my new-found relatives have told me, she always had 'ideas above her station' and thought a lot of herself, too. She had looks and she knew how to use them to get what she wanted. One of my most treasured possessions is a battered old black-and-white photograph of Mum. It was taken in the early 1960s and she looks very glamorous, very much a girl of the times with her bouffant hair-do. I examine the picture regularly and try to remember her as she was then, but it is so long ago. I look too to see if there is any resemblance between us. I want there to be, and although I know how much I look like my father I am pleased when other people see the photograph and comment that I am like her.

Mum met my dad through a friend with whom she had

been inside. This girl had a relative living down south and she invited Catherine to come and stay for a while after they were released. Mum apparently took up the invitation and went off to the village of Much Marcle on the Gloucestershire–Worcestershire border. Her pal was dating Dad's brother John and soon they were making up a regular foursome. My rebellious mother was obsessed with my father and wildly attracted by his strange gypsy looks and bushy brown hair. Nothing anybody said made any difference. She wanted him, and that was that.

But as the old-fashioned expression goes, Mum was no better than she should be. By the time she married Fred she was pregnant by someone else. I don't know if it was from an affair she had before she met Dad or while she was with him, or whether she was already in some way on the game. Whatever the truth, my sister Charmaine was certainly not Fred's. It was obvious to all because Charmaine was half-caste. Her real dad was of Asian extraction. The story goes that Mum was seeing an Asian chap who really loved her, but his family, who didn't approve, sent him back to his own country in disgrace. I don't know if he ever knew he had a daughter, or even that Mum was pregnant. Fred married Catherine, it is said, in the full knowledge that the child she was carrying wasn't his. I have even heard talk in the family that he married her because she was desperate and didn't want to go back to her family, who were also bound to disapprove of her condition.

So the first child to appear in my complicated family tree is Charmaine. Her parentage makes her my half-sister. In fact, although I have an enormous number of brothers and sisters – and probably even more I don't even know about – none of them are actually full blood relatives of mine. That has never mattered – I have always wanted to love and protect them all. Charmaine's birth, in March 1963, caused consternation in Much Marcle. The Swinging Sixties had not reached deepest Gloucestershire and the arrival of a half-caste child by an unknown father was greeted with much gossip. To avoid it Mum and Dad packed their bags and headed for mum's neck of the woods, Glasgow, and dad's new career as an ice-cream man.

I came along in 1964. I suppose we looked like any other family for a while, although we still lived on the wrong side of the tracks. There was something of an ice-cream war going on between various families in Glasgow at the time which caused a lot of tension. Some people thought others were pinching their routes and it got to be like a Mafia feud. They were a hard lot, and some carried knives, so I don't think it was a very safe profession.

It is hard for me to face this, at that time Mum must have been working as a prostitute. I don't know if she had established clients or worked the streets or clubs or what. Dad claimed she had a vicious black pimp but 60 per cent of what he said was always rubbish so I don't know quite what to believe. I long for more information about my mother. All my life I have felt that something was missing and I know now that it was a mother's love. I thought, and was often told, she had abandoned me and didn't love me. Now I know that she did care, and it does help to ease the hurt of all those years. Of course, the one person who could have told me a lot about her was my father, but I never trusted his version of events. Some of the things he told me about my mother made my blood run cold. Then I realised they were just more of his fantasies and instead I clung to the picture I had of her in my own mind.

When I was told that Dad had killed Mum I could not believe it. I always had this idea of them as wild, reckless and devoted lovers. I suppose the impression must have come from things my father told me, embroidered by my own imagination. I remember Dad showing me the tattoo on his arm, done in blue Indian ink. 'You see that? Your mum did that,' he told me, grinning. 'She did it when I was blind drunk one night. She wrote her name on my arm so no other woman would be in any doubt who I belonged to.' There, etched on his upper arm in capital letters, was the word 'Rena', the affectionate shortened version of Mum's name her family and Dad always used. He was quite proud of that tattoo; proud that she managed to do it without him knowing and that she wanted to put her mark on him. 'It will always be there,' he laughed. And after that, whenever the tattoo was mentioned, he would seem amused at the memory of how it came about.

One day when all this is over I want to sit down with my mum's family and spend the day talking about her. I want to know everything. I want to know what she was like as a kid and growing up. And most of all, I want to know what she was like as a mother. I want to hear all the stories most children know about their parents, the memories that fill in the gaps and prove you have roots. The impression I have of Mum has been built up partly from that photograph, maybe a little from memory and from what I have been told since. Relatives and neighbours in Glasgow used to think she was very glamorous and sophisticated. When she turned up to visit she looked like a movie star. There was never a hair out of place and her make-up was perfect. Dad, too, looked well groomed. He would always have a bit of cash on him and would give my cousins money to buy sweets. One of my aunts told me she would be standing in the kitchen in her dirty old apron and in would come Mum and Dad, all dolled up. Mum wih her beautiful hair, beautiful nails and really looking the part. Local kids used to think they were famous. I don't know where they got their money, but there was certainly a bit of wheeling and dealing going on.

There is one vague memory of my mum which I cling to in the hope that it truly happened. It is of the day she came back to get me. She was absent a lot in my early years, always flitting off here, there and everywhere; that's why I spent so much time with my dad and became so attached to him as a toddler. When Mum did her brief disappearing acts she always took Charmaine with her and left me with Dad. It's almost as if they had agreed that Charmaine was hers and I was Dad's. I don't know how old I was – I suppose I must have been very young.

I was playing quietly on my own in the living room of our home in Midland Road, Gloucester when the doorbell went. Rose went to answer it. I think Dad was out. Rose was out there for some time and I heard talking but I couldn't make out what was being said. So, like any curious child, I went and took a peek around the doorframe.

There was a woman standing talking to Rose. The contrast between them was extreme. The stranger was tall and elegant and she had her hair up, not in a bun, but in a sort of beehive like they used to wear in the sixties. Her hair was very blonde and set. In the snapshot I have of Mum she is dark, but the police have since told me that she used to dye her hair. I must have seen her to have that contradictory image of her as a blonde. I can't remember exactly what she was wearing, but she looked very smart. It was probably a smart suit with a shortish skirt. To me she looked elegant and nice. Rose, as usual, had no make-up on and was wearing trousers and a baggy top.

The woman smiled down at me. She said: 'Do you want to stay with your dad or do you want to come with me?'

I was confused. I didn't recognise her, and nobody gave me any explanation. I replied: 'I love my dad. I want to stay with him.'

The woman said nothing and went away. It was only afterwards that Rose told me: 'That was your mum.'

I don't know what I felt. She was almost a fictional character, whereas my dad was real and I loved him. So I stayed put. But the idea that Mum came back for me is comforting and I hope she will forgive me for not choosing her.

4

My Father's Family

Much has been written about why my dad did what he did, and any number of psychologists, professional and amateur, have had their say. It seems likely that his background and early relationships played their part. The rural community in which he grew up was isolated and insular. People say that even today there is a 'Much Marcle face', giving rise to the suggestion that inbreeding was once rife.

Incest and child abuse weren't discussed in those days the way they are now, but they was certainly a fact of life. Fred was abused by his own father and in his late teens he was questioned by the police after he got a thirteen-year-old girl pregnant. Members of the family acknowledge the sexual abuse but won't discuss it further. He was not bright or well educated, and repeated with his own family the pattern of his childhood and adolescence. He worshipped his mother and was devastated when she died aged only forty-four. Fred, who was then twenty-five, had doted on her, often confided in her, and respected her greatly. He spoke of her with a kind of reverence even when telling us how she kept the kids in line with an old-fashioned cuff around the ear.

Her death and the manner of it were something he never talked about. I can't be sure of the facts, but his mum, Daisy West, is said to have died while in hospital for a routine operation, appendix or gall bladder, I think. She was recovering well and had struck up a superficial friendship with a window-cleaner to whom she could wave from the window of her ward. One day, while waving back, he fell off his ladder and plunged several floors to his death. Daisy was so shocked she suffered a heart attack and joined him in the arms of the Almighty.

The history of my father's family has been much easier to trace than my mother's, mainly because I knew some of it from an early age and because we never lost touch with the West side of the family in the way we did with my mother's relatives. Once Mum had disappeared there was no contact with the Scottish connections, but Dad's brothers, sisters, uncles and aunts would pop up from time to time. From them I have pieced together some of the influences which shaped my father and later affected my own childhood.

As the stormclouds gathered over Europe and Britain prepared itself for another world war, in rural Gloucestershire my grandfather, Walter West, was busy falling in love with a pretty housemaid called Daisy Hannah Hill. Walter was employed as a farm labourer, providing much-needed food for the country, which prevented him from joining up. So while other men were going off to war, Walter was making the most of the lack of competition for the hand of the sharp-tongued Daisy.

Whether or not he was truly in love with her at the beginning I don't know, but he was certainly looking for a wife, having recently become a widower. At twenty-three, Walter, a shy and reserved man who used to walk along the lane with his head bowed, not meeting anyone's eye, had made an unlikely marriage to a woman old enough to be his mother, forty-five-year-old Gertrude Maddocks, to the amazement of the villagers and his own family. The couple were unable to have children, probably because of Gertrude's age, and planned to adopt a little boy from a local children's home. The two-year-old lad went to stay with them for a trial period while the paperwork was prepared. He was a pretty blond baby and Walter and Gertrude adored him. But the happy, if unconventional household fell apart on 7 June 1939, when Walter came home from work to find that Gertrude had collapsed and died. The child went back to the children's home and Walter began his search for a new partner.

It wasn't long before Daisy caught his eye. This time he went to the other extreme — Daisy was only sixteen. Their first meeting was at a major annual event for the village, the Much Marcle Show. The agricultural show, with its fruit, flowers and general produce competitions, was attended by everyone in the area. Daisy was showing off her needlework at one of the stands when Walter noticed her. For a shy man he worked quickly. After complimenting her on her handiwork he pursuaded her to accompany him out of the giant marquee for a ride on the swing boats.

It was the beginning of a typical rural courtship, and Walter wasted no time in making Daisy wife number two.

She was working for a wealthy Ledbury family called Gunter Jones and lived in during the week. On weekday evenings Walter would cycle three miles from the farm at Preston Cross to see her. At weekends he would call at her family home, a cottage called Cowley's opposite the cider factory which was the village's biggest claim to fame.

A close examination of dates suggests that they married in such a hurry for a reason as old as time, but if they did rush down the aisle because Daisy was pregnant, then at least Walter was very prompt at honouring his duty and popping the question. The wedding took place on 27 January 1940 at Much Marcle Parish Church. Walter was twenty-six and Daisy seventeen. Their first child, Violet, was born just over six months later, on 6 August 1940. Walter always claimed the baby came prematurely after his young wife received a shock. There had been an accident on the road near Veldt Cottages, where they were living, and a policeman came to the door looking for witnesses. For some unknown reason Daisy was frightened of the constable and went into labour that night, according to Walter. Whether this was a bit of rural folklore designed to account for the early arrival of the child made no difference to the fate of their firstborn. Violet died the following day.

Not long afterwards Walter went to work for another farmer. With the job came a tied home, Bickerton Cottage. Their next child, my father, Fred, was born there at 8.30 a.m. on 29 September 1941. He was baptised the following month at the church where his parents had been married. His christening card, still in our family's possession, was illuminated like a page from the Bible in gold, red, blue and green. One of four inscriptions on the corners of the card reads: 'He that believeth and is baptised shall be saved.'

Out of the Shadows

Soon after Fred's birth the family moved again, to 1 Moor Court Cottages in Much Marcle. My grandmother went on to produce her offspring with a regularity not uncommon at the time. John was born in October 1942; David Henry George in September 1943, but he died a month later. Daisy arrived in August 1944, Douglas in November 1946, Kathleen in November 1947 and Gwendoline, after a brief respite, in February 1951. The crowded life at Moor Court Cottages was marked by the mix of happiness and hardship which dogged the rural working classes in those days. When the children were young there were just three bedrooms but by the late 1950s an extension had been added which also provided a downstairs bathroom.

Walter worked at Moorcourt Farm, getting up at 4.30 a.m. and milking a dairy herd twice a day by hand. He had to get the full churns of milk up on to the road to await collection by eight o'clock every morning. In the winter he worked until the light failed and in the summer he might still be in the fields long after 9 p.m. Daisy and the other women in the village also worked the land. A lorry would come round the village to collect them and take them hop-picking, or sometimes currant-picking. I have always imagined it to have been like an episode of *The Darling Buds of May* on television, though I'm sure in reality it was very hard work.

Even the smallest children joined in. If they wanted an ice-cream, they had to pick enough hops or currants to earn it. Dad and all my uncles and aunts would go hop-picking in the school holidays and at the end of the summer it would be time for hay-making and harvesting. They thought it was all great fun. They would help by rolling the bales across the field for the adults to stack up. The harvesting was done with an old-style binder and as soon as the kids got home from school they would change their clothes, grab a stick and be off to catch the rabbits uncovered by the reaping. The younger ones weren't allowed to go rabbiting, but of course Dad was always there. Twenty or thirty village kids would be around the edge of the field looking for rabbits. When the farmer stopped the machine in the middle of the field there would be one big patch of corn left. As the rabbits came out the kids would hit them with their sticks. Some used broken pick-axe handles, others walking sticks or whatever they could get their hands on. As the rabbits were caught they were thrown on the binder in a heap and when it was all over the farmer used to dish them out. If there were any left over the larger families, like Dads's, were given one or two extra. They would take them home to Daisy, who roasted them or made rabbit stew.

My uncles tell a story about village lad who took his little terrier rabbiting with him. He put his dog in to the corn but as the crop rattled and the dog came out again my Uncle John hit it, thinking it was a rabbit. They had to rush the poor creature down to the brook two fields away to revive it.

Money was short and the family lived off what they could get, but there were other perks, besides the rabbits, which came from living in the country and working on a farm. Walter always had plenty of fresh milk with which to feed his growing family. There was a little bit of land with Bickerton Cottage as well, and that provided another source of food. The family kept their own pig in a sty in the backyard, and when it was ready it would be killed by a local slaughterman who came up to the house on a Saturday. Then the pig would be salted and hung up to make bacon, which would last for almost a year.

My grandfather also had an allotment in the village where

he grew peas and beans. They had their own chickens, too, which Daisy and the kids looked after. They produced fresh eggs and the occasional pot-boiler. One of the hens was always killed for Christmas and in later years ducks and geese were kept, which meant delicious roast goose for Christmas lunch. Daisy made all the family's bread.

The six children had to help with the chores from quite a young age and as they got older they were given more responsible jobs. I suppose everyone had to do their bit, otherwise with eight people living in one small cottage, it would have been chaos. The older children, who included dad of course, had to help Walter with the milking. My grandmother could also milk a cow and mucked in if necessary. The first domestic task of the day generally went to the boys, and that was to get in the coal and wood from outside. There was a small grate in the sitting room and a big open fire with a black leaded grate in the kitchen, with an oven on the side. They were the only source of heat in the cottage; there was none at all upstairs. In the winter Daisy would put the old-style stone hot-water bottles in the beds to warm them up. Evenings, when the children were young, would be spend playing cards or dominos in front of the fire. It was a very strong family circle and they did everything together, whether it was working or enjoying themselves.

Twice a year my grandparents, my father, and all my uncles and aunts would go on a day's coach trip to Barry Island in South Wales, in May, before potato-picking. Almost everyone in the village went. They would all have a good sing-song on the bus and go for a paddle in the sea when they got there. Then there was the funfair and the amusements, a picnic on the beach and perhaps a bag of chips before heading home.

Although I have quite a detailed picture of my father's

childhood, he never told me much about it himself. Most of the stories have been related over the years by uncles and aunts. But I have always known Dad was my grandmother's favourite. I think she tried to treat all the kids the same, but Fred, or Freddie as the family called him then, her firstborn son, was her blue-eyed boy. He could wriggle out of doing his chores if he tried really hard, and he often did, but he still had to keep in line. Daisy was quite capable of cuffing him round the ear if she felt he deserved it.

As the boys became young men and went off on their own in the evenings they still had pretty strict rules to adhere to. They were told what time they had to be back and my grandmother used to stay up until the last one came in. The rules applied right up until the time they got married. If anyone was a few minutes late he would get the rough side of his mother's tongue, and if she judged that they had badly transgressed, the worst threat was that she would tell their father. If that happened, they made themselves scarce. Walter's favourite method of punishment was a beating with a leather belt, and he wasn't afraid to use it.

Daisy was more likely to use her hand or, on occasions, a shovel – as my dad once found to his cost. He was messing around with a wooden sword which his father had made for him for a school play. Dad and Uncle John were larking about and play-fighting and John made a dive for the kitchen and shut the door. Fred pulled it open a crack and poked the sword violently through the gap. 'I gotcha. I gotcha!' he yelled. But he hadn't. He had got Daisy, right in the stomach. She was on her way out for a shovelful of coal, so he got the shovel full-force.

My father was a competitive youngster at the Much Marcle village school, but apparently he didn't excel at team games.

He was quite happy to play with the family at home, but at school he preferred individual pursuits. He was a good runner and represented the school in inter-school sports days, but he didn't go much on cricket or soccer.

He did, however, have artistic skills. He was a very good carpenter, and was in his element if someone gave him a piece of wood to carve. He was always making things for his mother. Once he made her a footstool, and another time a book cabinet, although he was barely able to read and write himself. He was also good at drawing and spent a lot of time sketching. When he was on remand I took him a sketchpad and pencils, a birthday present from his grandchildren.

It may be hard to believe, but my father wasn't a violent boy, either. His brothers say he wouldn't stick up for himself. He wasn't a fighter and had a really long fuse. Apparently you could have a really good go at him before he would think of fighting back, unlike his brother John, who always had his fists ready. He wasn't exactly timid, though. He was quite happy to mix with other youngsters and from a very early age he was one for chatting up the girls. Yet he never wanted to defend himself and had a reputation for lacking bottle. None of the other West kids were like that. Even the girls would stand up for themselves.

Fred had quite a sensitive nature. When he was about fifteen he had an air rifle and used to shoot at a target in a tree. One day he was showing off and pretended to shoot at a bird. He wasn't much of a shot and didn't think for a moment he would hit it, but he did, and he blew it to pieces. He got what for from his mother, but according to the rest of the family he genuinely felt bad enough about hitting it anyway.

When Dad left school he got a job as a farm labourer,

working alongside his father. At about the same time he got his first motorbike and his first girlfriend. She was a lass called Elsie who lived in the village. He was on his way home from her house one night when he had a terrible accident. He went round a bend too fast on the road between Fingerpost Field and Moorcourt Cottages and hit a pedestrian head-on. As for my dad, the way he told it, they rushed him to hospital, where he 'died' on the operating table. He claimed the doctors pronounced him dead and sent him down to the mortuary. The slab was so cold it started his heart going again and he was was taken back to the operating theatre at top speed. Who knows whether it is true, but if so I expect there are a lot of people who wish the slab had been warmer. Dad always told me when I was little that the surgeons had had to rebuild his face. He said one side was plastic and that he had a metal plate in his head. My uncles and aunts say he was certainly knocked out cold and had bad concussion. He was in hospital for over a week and had to wear a caliper with two metal bars on his leg for two months.

Fred had promised his mum that if he ever had a bad accident on the bike he would sell it, so he did. Then he passed his driving test and he and Uncle John bought a car between them. But it was mostly Dad who used to disappear in it for hours on end – usually with some girl, it was generally supposed. He had a reputation for promising the rest of the family a lift, dropping them off somewhere, maybe the cinema in Ross-on-Wye, and then not coming back at the time arranged. He would always turn up in the end, but they had to do a lot of hanging around waiting for him. It caused no end of rows and Daisy would get after him for it. He would be very helpful for a day or two, but then he'd slide back to his old ways again.

Out of the Shadows

My uncles say Dad had a very quiet approach to the girls in his younger days. He never made a big song and dance about it, but if he saw a girl he liked he went straight over and chatted her up. He obviously had quite a high success rate, but there was one night when he pushed his luck a little too far.

He had given his mum and brother John a lift to Newent and then drove back to a local youth club in Ledbury. He was about eighteen or nineteen at the time. He was trying a chat-up line on a young woman there and had persuaded her to go out on to the fire escape with him 'for some fresh air'. The air wasn't the only thing that was fresh: Dad tried to put his hand up the girl's skirt. Nobody knows if she meant to do it, but she shoved him down the fire escape and he fell head-first quite some distance. He was out cold for twenty-four hours after another bang on the head. The doctors examined him and said he was fine, and according to the family he was the same man after the accident as before. It seemed to have no effect on his personality.

5

The Day I Met Rose

The day I first met Rose, I snubbed her in favour of my breakfast. I was five years old and felt I had my priorities right. The early-morning meal in the children's home where I was living — cornflakes sprinkled with sugar and cold milk topped up with hot water — was far more important than the new girlfriend my dad had brought to be introduced to me. It was the one and only time I ever got away with antagonising Rose. Today it gives me a small sense of satisfaction. At the time I was interested only in where the next meal was coming from.

I was in the children's home in Gloucester because Dad had told the social services that his wife had left him and he could not work full-time and cope with two young children alone. I don't think Charmaine was with me, but our social services records show that we both spent time in a number of foster homes in the Cheltenham and Gloucester areas, so perhaps she was still in one of those. The day's routine was just like any other and it was barely disturbed by the visit from my father and his new girlfriend. I slept in a narrow bed in a dormitory with a lot of other little children. After washing and dressing ourselves, we ran downstairs to the dining room to have our breakfast.

This particular morning, as I was coming down the huge, wide staircase, which always reminded me of something out of a film, I saw my father at the bottom. He had someone with him. He called to me: 'Anna-Marie, it's your dad. Come and see your dad.' I was always pleased to see him and smiled and quickened my step on the bare boards.

'Dad. Hello, Dad.'

Then I became fully aware of the young woman with him. I gave her little more than a cursory glance, though I took in her youth — she was about sixteen — and her long, dark hair. She looked apprehensive and tried a small smile, which came out as more of a grimace. I didn't meet her eyes; instead I turned back to my father. I don't remember what I thought, but I know I ignored Rose completely.

'Aren't you pleased to see your dad? I've brought someone to meet you.'

Before he could get out another word I told him, 'I can't stop. I'll miss my breakfast.'

And without even a goodbye I trotted off to the dining room, leaving them standing in the huge hallway looking lost. I don't know how Dad explained my behaviour, and I don't really understand why I did it. Normally I would have been delighted by a visit from my much-loved father, but that day all I wanted was my cornflakes.

Of course, they tried again with another visit, and that one was much more successful. For a start they brought a present with them. It was a doll, the kind of old-fashioned doll you don't see these days. She had a switch on her back and you laid her on her tummy and she wriggled and crawled. She had long blonde hair, and I recall holding her by those bright tresses in the way five-year-olds do. I can't remember what I called her but I can still remember her plasticky smell. Whenever I come across the smell of that particular kind of plastic it immediately takes me back. It was the only present I ever received from Rose that wasn't a bribe or accompanied by a threat. I used to cuddle it a lot. I think I still had it after I left the children's home, but what happened to it eventually I don't know. It's strange, because that doll was one of the few toys I ever had and I should have treasured it, but although I loved it at first I must have cast it aside at some point.

Dad first handed Charmaine and me over to the social services on 14 December 1965. My parents had separated in March 1965 and Dad had brought us back to the West Country. Charmaine was two and a half and I was just a year old. A friend of my mother's, from Scotland, Anne McFall, looked after us for a while. Dad employed her as a kind of nanny. We all lived in a mobile home at the Timberland Caravan Park in Brockworth, a suburb of Gloucester.

I was too young to recall anything much about Anne. She disappeared in May 1967 when she was eighteen years old and more than six months' pregnant. The baby is suspected to have been my father's. Anne's body was discovered twenty-seven years later buried in Fingerpost Field in Much Marcle, and my father was charged with her murder. When I visited him in prison a few months before his death, he told me she was the one woman he had truly loved and implicated my mother in her murder. I didn't believe him.

The social services records, which were handed over to

the police as part of their inquiry, show that Charmaine and I were often separated during the time we were in care. They also reveal that Fred and our mother visited us. The last recorded visit by our mum was made to Charmaine at the beginning of 1970. By that time I had been handed back to Dad and Rose and we were all living in Cheltenham. In March 1970, Dad collected Charmaine and not long afterwards we moved to Midland Road.

I remember living in the flat there and I remember Dad disappearing for a while. I'm not sure if at that age I realised he was in prison, but nonetheless the day we went to visit him there is clear in my mind. He was in Leyhill Open Prison, serving time for fraud. Rose and I went to see him on sports day. I was in the egg-and-spoon race, but I didn't do very well because I kept dropping the egg. I can still see the open expanse of grass where the games took place and remember it as a hot, sunny afternoon. I was happy because I was seeing my dad, he was encouraging me to do well and he seemed genuinely pleased to see us all. I couldn't work out what he was doing there or why he didn't come home with us. I suppose I just thought it was some sort of job he was doing, and besides, he was home soon enough.

In those days I viewed Rose as little more than a schoolgirl besotted with my dad and unable to cope with the role of stepmother to two difficult children. At least, she regularly told us we were difficult, and I don't suppose someone who was little more than a child herself found us easy to manage. Charmaine probably made things worse by frequently voicing her obsession that her real mum would be coming back to claim her any day. For my part, I didn't help by constantly trying to win the attention of my beloved dad. On top of all of this, it wasn't long before Rose was pregnant with her first child: my half-sister Heather.

Rose and Dad met when she was working in a local cake shop. I expect he chatted her up — that sounds like Dad. Back then he was known as a lovable bloke who would do anything for anybody. He could be dead charming when he wanted to be, and I expect he found Rose, then only fifteen, a very easy target. Her worried parents didn't approve at all and placed her in the care of the social services. She was, by all accounts, already a bit of a handful. But as soon as she reached sixteen, only a matter of weeks after she was taken into care, she was legally allowed to leave, and leave she did, heading straight for my Dad's waiting arms.

So there we all were: Dad with this new young girlfriend and two children, all in the flat in Midland Road. I don't suppose we ever looked like a normal family, with Charmaine's mixed ancestry and both of us obviously too old to be Rose's, and Dad so much older than his new love. I imagine plenty of other unusual families who have got by in a fairly ordinary fashion but it wasn't the case in our house. For a start Charmaine hated Rose and told her so. She would go out of her way to antagonise and aggravate our volatile stepmother. She never missed a chance to remind Rose about our real mother. We had been ordered by Dad to call Rose 'Mum', but neither of us wanted to and it caused enormous problems.

It was obvious from the word go that Rose had a hell of a temper and was not able to control it. She made us do most of the household chores despite our ages and if we didn't do them right she erupted. Doing them right, of course, meant doing them Rose's way: there was no other. If you did it wrong, you got a hiding. Our new stepmother didn't try to hide the beatings from Dad. It was rare for him to lose his temper with us or hit us himself, but he never, ever objected to Rose doing so. In later years his only comment would be: 'Make sure you hit them where it doesn't show.'

There are for too many incidents involving Rose's violent streak to document them all, but some stand out more than others. One I checked recently with my medical records, and sure enough, there it was. The notes held at my doctor's surgery revealed that I had a number of stitches in a head wound after a 'fall', a favourite euphemism for an injury inflicted by Rose. It happened one breakfast time as Charmaine and I were getting ready for school. As usual big sister was taking her time over the chores and capitalising on an opportunity to wind up our stepmother. But it was me who suffered for it on that occasion.

Rose snapped at us: 'Come on. You've had your breakfast. Wash the plates up. Get off your backsides and do it.'

Charmaine just looked at her with dumb insolence. Then she slowly rose from the table, scraping her chair as loudly as possible. With no sense of urgency, she picked up her plate and headed for the sink.

Rose yelled: 'Move it!' adding a few choice swearwords.

Charmaine stuck out her bottom lip. 'My real mother wouldn't swear or shout at us,' she told Rose.

I could sense trouble brewing and queued up quickly behind my sister at the sink to wash my bowl too. But I couldn't get to the tap because Charmaine was idly playing with her bowl in the washing-up water. She was having a good old mess with it. Rose I could tell was getting flustered and irate.

She snapped at me: 'What are you doing there?'

'I'm waiting to wash my plate,' I told her, my voice barely

Out of the Shadows

audible. She snatched the plate from me and lashed out, breaking it across my head in one movement.

The blow was severe and it hurt. It was meant to. The result was a deep and bloody gash on the side of my head. I don't remember the trip to the doctor or who took me, but I can recall having the stitches and I have never forgotten the pain.

As time went on Rose's violence knew no bounds. It was hard to pinpoint what set it off or when it was coming. Often there seemed no reason for it, and no one person was either responsible for it or at the receiving end. She could be just as violent towards my father as she was towards the younger members of the family. Her wrath was indiscriminate, with one exception – the babies. Rose absolutely adored children until they were about one year old. She loved the helplessness of them and she loved to do things for them. If you saw her with a tiny infant you would have thought she was the world's best mother. She would hold him, cuddle him, rock him and coo over him. But the moment children developed any signs of independence, such as crawling, walking, or talking, things changed. Then they became a nuisance and would feel the sharp end of her tongue and her temper.

Although she was violent towards all the children in the family at one time or another she was never as bad with her own as she was with Charmaine and me. Once Charmaine had disappeared, of course, I was the sole whipping girl. I came to believe quite early on that I deserved the beatings and was as evil, awkward and difficult as she claimed. I loved the other children so much and hated to see them hurt that I would interfere on their behalf, even though I knew she would transfer her rage from them to me. I was so used to it that it almost ceased to matter. Charmaine, in some ways, probably did the same for me, although perhaps not intentionally. It was in her nature to rebel and part of her stoic character to accept her punishment.

We were opposites in many ways but we were both very self-contained children. We occasionally played together and shared a bedroom but we didn't often confide in each other. Our upbringing made us deep and secretive and neither of us gave much away. There was little time anyway for children's games. We were too busy doing the housework for Rose. We would set and prepare the table for meals, help with the cooking, wash up, tidy our rooms and the rest of the house and do most of the washing and ironing. When things got tough Charmaine would talk wistfully to me about this fairy-godmother-type creature who would one day be back to rescue her and take her off to a happier life. She never seemed to think our mother would want to take me too, just her.

I have seen old photographs of Charmaine since the police began their investigation into Fred and Rose, but I remembered what she looked like anyway. In my mind she remains as she was when I last saw her, when was about six and she was nearly eight. She was darker than me, with an olive complexion, a Legacy of her Asian father. She had big, beautiful brown eyes and long, dark shiny black hair. She was tall and matchstick thin. She was a very pretty child and would have grown up to be a stunning young woman.

We went to school together for a brief period but we were in different classes. The police think our mother sometimes used to intercept Charmaine on the way to school and take her off for the day. This probably made Rose's story that she had gone off to live with Rena even more convincing. No one bothered to look for her and the school register was simply marked, 'Moved away.'

* * *

Out of the Shadows

After the police found my sister's body at the house in Midland Road almost three months after they discovered Heather's, I went back there to lay some flowers in her memory as I had done for my younger sister. I attatched a note to the bouquet. 'To my sister Charmaine. We played, we cried, we laughed and sang — but how I've prayed we'd be together again. Missing you so very much. Will always love and remember you. All my fondest love, Anna-Marie.'

I stood in the garden, tears blinding my view for an instant, and gazed at the house. A softly spoken policeman showed me the spot in the garden where her remains had been found, just by the back door. There is a kitchen extension there now, but it wasn't there when we were kids. I looked to my right and there was our bedroom window. We used to share that room. It had two single beds: Charmaine's was under the window and mine was right against the wall. As I stared up at the window, in my mind's eye I could see the two of us cuddled up under the blankets on dark winter nights. The window, above my sister's bed, would rattle in the wind. It looked like the same window, even now. Charmaine would shudder and say to me: 'Anna-Marie, Anna-Marie, the witches are trying to get in. They're going to get us.'

We would snuggle even deeper under the blankets for protection, frightening ourselves to death as the wind howled outside. Poor little kid: she used to get so frightened. I hate to think of the terror she must have felt and the suffering she went through before she died. I can see us now in that bare little room, two wide-eyed mites frightened of the witches outside and not realising evil was already in the house sleeping just down the hall.

6

My Sister Charmaine

Charmaine was nearly eight when she disappeared; I would have been six or seven and Heather just a few months old. Rose was just seventeen. It happened when Dad was in Leyhill Prison, where he was banged up from 4 December 1970. He had been sentenced to ten months but actually served just under seven months. The police found it difficult to pinpoint exactly when my sister was killed and I wasn't able to help much because I was so young at the time.

Hospital records show that Charmaine had been treated for an ankle injury on 28 March 1971. The notes don't specify what caused the puncture wound: it was simply put down as a household accident, but I have little doubt that Rose would have been responsible. It must have been quite serious for her to take Charmaine to a doctor. The police originally accused my father of murdering Charmaine but after he was found hanged in prison they charged Rose. The evidence pointed strongly to my stepmother. Documents found in the attic at Cromwell Street, including letters between Dad and Rose and a prison pre-release record, proved that Fred was still inside when Charmaine vanished, although he was freed soon afterwards.

When her body was dug up in the garden on 4 May 1994 there were bits of coal around it. It seems likely that Rose went too far one day, killed her and dumped her body in our old coal shed. When Dad came home he must have moved the body and buried it out the back.

Charmaine was found under the kitchen extension added after we left Midland Road. She had been buried on her back with her spine curved forward and her arms outstretched. Professor Bernard Knight who examined the body at the site, said that her legs might have been cut off at hip level, or perhaps the body had been disturbed by building work. As most of Dad's and Rose's victims had been carved up at the hip I suspect it was their work. Charmaine was described as lying in an almost foetal position. The bits of coal indicated that she had not originally been concealed in her final resting-place. As with the other victims, no cause of death could be determined because the remains were so old. I just hope she didn't suffer in death as much as she had already done in life.

When the press broke the story about Charmaine's body being found, a witness came forward who helped them work out roughly when she must have been killed. The woman had been a neighbour of ours in Midland Road. We occupied the ground-floor flat and she lived on the top floor. Mrs Shirley Giles, her husband and their two daughters, Tracey and Janet, moved to Midland Road some time in 1970. They were buying their own house and needed somewhere to live while the deal went through. They stayed there until January the following year.

I remember Tracey and Janet. It was wonderful for me and Charmaine to have two pals to play with. Sometimes we went to their flat and occasionally they came to ours. Charmaine and Tracey became best friends and were almost inseparable. They used to sit and giggle together and hold hands and generally behave as little girls do. I was younger and felt a bit left out. They did let me play with them quite a bit, but they were very close.

When the police interviewed Mrs Giles in June 1994, she told them: 'Rose would comment that she could not cope with Charmaine. My impression was that Anne Marie had been browbeaten whereas Charmaine had a rebellious nature. Anne Marie was pretty timid; Rose said she could cope with her. She was no problem.' Mrs Giles added that she felt Rose could not curb and control my sister in the way she wanted. By the time the Giles family were ready to move out, Rose was saying that she could not wait to get rid of Charmaine. She told our neighbour that she was waiting for the child's mother to arrive and take her away. 'I told Rose that Charmaine and Anne Marie should not be separated,' Mrs Giles said in her statement.

She recalled the day she and her family moved out and into their new home in Cinderford. 'Charmaine and Tracey were hugging one another and in tears.' She remembered, too, the day she came back to see us all, bringing Tracey along with her new baby sister, Claire. It was April 1971. Fred, she said, was still in prison. 'Rose let us in and said Charmaine was no longer with them. Her mother had come to Midland Road and taken her to Bristol. My daughter Tracey cried and Anne Marie comforted her.'

Tracey too was interviewed by the police in 1994, and although she was only a child when her playmate vanished she had some vivid memories. Charmaine, she told the detectives, had become her best friend. She described me as 'always quiet, and she seemed like Charmaine's shadow'. The day Tracey returned to Midland Road to visit us was etched in her mind. She remembered her tears when she realised she would never see Charmaine again and what Rose had said as she sobbed in dismay. 'She's gone to live with her mother, and bloody good riddance.'

Tracey told the police of another incident in Midland Road which painted a picture of our life there which I could not. It had stayed with her all her life, but to me it was barely memorable – just another day in our life with our stepmother. Her mum had run out of milk and sent her daughter to borrow some from the Wests for the family's breakfast cereal. Tracey trotted happily downstairs to the ground floor, armed with an empty jug.

> I knocked at the door and went in. I barged straight in and stopped. Charmaine was standing on an old wooden kitchen chair. She seemed calm and unconcerned. Her hands were behind her back with a belt tight around the wrists. The image is clear in my mind. The lady with long hair was standing there with a large wooden spoon. I was very shocked and upset. Anne Marie was standing by the door, expressionless.

I'm sure it happened, but it doesn't stand out in my mind. It was just another beating from Rose for one of us.

One day I came home from school to be told by Rose that Charmaine had gone off with her mother. I knew better than to question my stepmother and simply accepted what she said as fact. I missed my sister. We had been very different, but at least when she was there I had an ally. I didn't pine for her too much because I knew how much she wanted to be with Mum and I felt that now she would be happy. I think I must have become even more withdrawn after she'd gone. To make up for her absence I lavished my affection on my baby sister Heather.

I never brought up the subject of Charmaine with Rose, but some months later, when my father came home, I tried gently and tactfully to mention it to him. We were sitting at the kitchen table having a cup of tea and Rose was out of the room. I reckoned it was safe to take the risk. Dad leaned back in his chair and knocked some ash off the end of his cigarette. 'Yes. She's gone off with her mum. She came for her.'

I considered this carefully, checked that Rose wasn't on her way back and chanced: 'What about me, Dad? Did she want to take me?'

My father grinned. 'No. She wouldn't want you, love. You're the wrong colour.'

I didn't understand what he meant, but I didn't push it. My face must have given away my confusion, because he laughed and ruffled my hair. 'Don't you worry darlin'. I love you, even if your mum don't. You love your dad and your dad loves you, so it don't matter.'

Not long after Dad came home and some time after Charmaine went missing, we moved to 25 Cromwell Street, an address I am sure has already gone down in history along with other infamous homes such as 10 Rillington Place. But to me then it was just a new home, one which Dad had already spent a lot of time doing up. He was working for a local property-owner, a Polish man called Mr Zigman, who didn't speak much English and had also been our landlord at Midland Road. He's dead now.

It was 1972, and at first Dad rented the house but later he got a mortgage from the local council to buy it. I don't know how he afforded it, but he raised the deposit and in we moved. It was bigger than our previous home and had a big garden. It was like an orchard with beautiful apple and pear trees, five in all. I loved them, but Dad cut them down.

A few months before we moved to Cromwell Street Dad married Rose. It was 29 January 1972, and on his marriage certificate he described himself as a bachelor. There is no record of him ever having divorced my mother, but of course he knew she was dead and lying beneath the earth in a field in Much Marcle.

It was a strange kind of wedding. Dad came home from work one day and barely had time to change out of his working clothes before he and Rose dashed out of the house and along to the register office in Gloucester. They didn't make a big thing of it, they just went and did it. Five months later, on 1 June 1972, along came another half-sister. Perhaps because of the timing of her birth they called her Mae June. Now there was Dad, Rose and we three girls living in the three-storey town-centre semi. I say three-storey, but if you count the cellar there were four floors. There were three ways to gain access to the cellar. One was from the front garden, through an entrance underneath what much later became Mae's bedroom. This was hardly ever used. There was another way in at the back of the house via some stairs which originally came from the back garden, but later, after the extension was built, led down from the living room, and there was a main basement entrance from the main stairwell in the middle of the house.

It was an extensive lower ground floor, and one of the first areas of the house on which Fred set to work. It was to become the younger children's bedroom and eventually the setting for my wedding reception, but in those early years it was Fred and Rose's torture chamber, a prison where God knows how many young women suffered (I believe I was the first) and a macabre grave for the victims of a madman and his evil partner in crime.

I was nearly eight when we moved to Cromwell Street. I was excited about the huge new house and thrilled to have my beloved father home for good. I would try so hard to please him and would be over the moon if I achieved the ultimate – his praise and attention. But although I sometimes managed this, minutes later he would seem unconcerned when Rose chastised me for nothing or belted me around the head in a fit of temper. She was very jealous of his time and affection. A kindly word from my dad was often followed by a thump from Rose. If I did dare to complain to my father he would simply say: 'Your mum is doing that because she loves you. It's for your own good.'

I tried very hard to believe him because I wanted Rose to love me since it would please my dad. I tried hard, too, to do what she wanted, when she wanted it and in the way she wanted it done. But there was no pleasing her and I came to realise that my greatest crime was to be Dad's daughter by another woman. I had taken over Charmaine's role as the 'difficult' child.

Rose made no attempt to hide her cruel streak and my father's indifference, which bordered an active participation, made it unnecessary anyway. One afternoon, not long after we had moved into Cromwell Street, Rose ordered me to make tea for them and some visitors. I was used to boiling the kettle despite my age, and I brewed up and poured the tea into four cups. I put them on a tray and, with great care, headed for the living room. There was an extension to the room with some steps leading up to it, and I had to balance the heavy tray and watch where I was going at the same time. Unfortunately, I tripped on the steps and the scalding hot tea went all over me. Fred and Rose just sat there and laughed like anything. I was quite badly burned but they didn't offer to help. They just made me pick everything up and start all over again.

If Rose had had her way I would never have gone to school. I would have stayed at home to be her skivvy and look after the children which she produced with great regularity. But the alternative would undoubtedly mean interference from the authorities, so I was packed off to St James's Infants School every day more to prevent anyone from turning up at Cromwell Street asking about me than to get an education. I was given very little encouragement with my schoolwork at any time in my life, but I do remember when Rose tried to teach me how to tell the time. We sat around the kitchen table and she had a wooden toy clock with which she explained the mysteries of hours and minutes.

I got the hang of it quite quickly – it paid to be a bit quick off the mark in our house. But although I recognised full hours and the half-past bits I kept confusing the minutes to the hour with the minutes past. Every time I got it wrong Rose belted me across the head with her hand or the wooden clock. By the end of the day I could beat Big Ben at telling the time, although I certainly wouldn't recommend this as a teaching method.

We lived in a vacuum at Cromwell Street. No one was

Out of the Shadows

allowed in without Dad's or Rose's permission, not even our playmates from school. The house was protected by big iron gates which were meant to keep strangers out and us in. Callers had to ring one of two buzzers on the gates to get anyone to the front door a yard or two away. One of the bells was for general callers, the second for Rose's own private visitors. Dad always used to tell me: 'We don't want to have anything to do with people outside. We don't need them. There are people out there who will hurt you. You're safe inside them gates. You're with people who will protect you.'

I guess what he meant was that there were people outside those gates who would stop him and Rose enjoying their own menacing and sado-masochistic brand of fun. But as a child I believed him because I had no yardstick by which to judge him.

We shared our life at Cromwell Street with a never-ending string of lodgers. The house was quite large, and split into flats and bedsits. There were always different tenants. I don't know how they found out there was accommodation available — I expect it was by word of mouth. Dad would often bring home people he had met. No one stayed that long. I don't know if any of the people who stayed at our house ever suspected what was happening there. I have often wondered if they guessed I was being abused. Some, as will be obvious, knew and were involved, but surely there must have been some normal people in all that time who could have helped me. Perhaps anybody who came close to the truth was dealt with by Fred and Rose.

Rose and Dad were both well known in the area. They used to drink in a lot of the rough pubs nearby. The house is in the centre of Gloucester, so there were plenty of places to choose from. They went regularly to a local drinking club frequented by a lot of West Indians. They never worried about leaving the children alone. If they fancied going out, they just went. I suppose I was babysitting for the rest of the family from the age of about ten.

In those days the family rooms at Cromwell Street were downstairs and the rented rooms were all upstairs. At one time all the lodgers were men and at another there were just women. Sometimes it would be a mixed bunch. I remember when there were a few hippy types staying. They would get a bit wild and smash things up, but generally it never bothered us because it was rare for the lodgers to come into our part of the house. We didn't really associate with them. We had our own separate bathroom and kitchen and the lodgers had little kitchens on the landing of each of the two upper floors. They all had to share one bathroom on the middle floor. I hated our bathroom downstairs because it didn't have a lock and anybody could walk in when you were having a bath. I used to be in and out of the water as quickly as possible so that no one would see me. There was no privacy whatsoever in the house – it was all so open. At one time my sisters and I used to sleep in part of the living room, which was just curtained off from the rest of the room. We had bunk beds and I had the bottom one.

If you complained Rose would sneer: 'We made you and what you've got, we've given you. So if we want to look at it, we will.'

I spent my life trying to keep out of Rose's way and to avoid antagonising her, but it was an impossible job. I remember taking a beating because she had lost a tea towel. She was in the living room, going round and round in circles, yelling 'Tea towel, tea towel!' and I just didn't get it to her quickly enough. I got belted, too, for not stirring the gravy in the right way and not mashing the potatoes properly. Sometimes you felt the back of her hand but if she wanted to give you a good going-over she would grab the nearest weapon so that she didn't hurt herself. I was hit across the head with a broom on more than one occasion and I still have a small scar where she knifed my hand.

It was as if she had mental black-outs, almost as if she didn't know she was doing it. When she had finished, she might look at you and say: 'Your fucking fault. You should have done it properly.' On other occasions she wouldn't speak; she'd just carry on with what she was doing as if nothing had happened.

7

Raped By My Father

I was eight years old when my father raped me. Rose helped him. The day is branded on my memory forever and contains scenes even the worst video-nasty director would not contemplate filming.

Although I was used to the violence in our household, directed mostly at me, I had no real fear the day Dad and Rose led me down to the basement of our home in Cromwell Street. It was quite dark and dingy but Dad used it occasionally as a workshop then and at that time, in 1972, it was split into three sections. At the very back there were lots of Dad's tools and the front section was starting to be used as a play area for the children. As you went downstairs into the basement you had to duck your head because the ceiling was very low at that point. Dad had put some kind of board he had made between the sections, where there might have been glass, and had drilled air-holes in it.

We went down the stairs, the three of us, and I noticed

a number of items on the floor. I still wasn't really worried because I didn't know what they were. I had been in the playroom section before but had never actually played there — I was kept too busy doing the housework for that. As the three of us stood at the bottom of the stairs I suddenly began to get nervous. All of a sudden, there was an atmosphere I couldn't fathom.

I asked my father: 'Dad, what's going on? What are you doing?' I repeated the question a couple of times but they said nothing, just looked at each other. Rose had a strange smirk on her face as if she was really going to enjoy herself but wasn't going to say why.

My father said: 'Just do as you are told. Take your clothes off and put them on the floor. Go on, get on with it.'

I didn't understand but I started to do it anyway. I obviously wasn't quick enough for Rose. Almost in one movement she just ripped my cotton summer dress right off me. 'You heard your father. Get that off.' The material ripped as she spoke and she threw it on the floor.

The pair of them grabbed hold of me and pinned me down. I was on some kind of old mattress. I started to cry and said once again: 'What are you doing?'

'Just shut up and be quiet,' Rose spat the words out and laughed as I struggled.

One of them held me while the other assembled the things on the floor. I could see a glass mixing bowl with water in it, some black tape, some strips of torn cotton sheets and an object I later learned was a vibrator. My father used the black sticky tape, the kind of stuff you use to put around carpets, to bind my hands together. The sheeting was to secure my hands and arms to an iron object above my head.

I was absolutely terrified. I was eight years old and had

Out of the Shadows

no understanding of what was about to happen to me, but I knew it was something awful and that it was going to hurt. My father said very little but Rose was encouraging him to get on with it. I was struggling so much that she sat on my head to keep me still and I started to panic because I couldn't breathe. She was scratching and pawing at me. She had an evil look in her eye. There was no emotion at all, just that all-consuming look of pure evil. I was screaming and crying so much it hurt me. Dad shouted at Rose, 'Can't you hold her?' And she got some more of the sheeting and put it around my mouth as a gag.

Just before she did I screamed at my father: 'Why are you doing this, Dad? It hurts!' His reply was chilling but made little sense to me then. He told me: 'Shut up. It is going to help you in later life. I'm just doing what all fathers have to do. It's a normal thing, so stop carrying on. This will make sure you get a husband when you're older. You'll be ready for him and you'll be able to have children.'

I remember the pain as they inserted something inside me. It hurt so much I just wanted to die. They pulled my legs open and secured them and I remember looking at the glass bowl on the floor and it was all red. It frightened me. Whatever they were doing seemed to take forever and the pain was so bad I almost lost conciousness.

After a while – I have no idea how long the ordeal lasted – they left me. They just upped and went, leaving me bound hand and foot, but without my gag, and went back into the main part of the house. The removal of the gag meant I could breathe properly again but my screams and sobbing went unnoticed. My DIY expert father had soundproofed the basement.

I lay motionless for what seemed an age. My pain was

masked by a fear that they would come back and start all over again. I was shivering from the cold in the cellar and from sheer fright. I couldn't take my eyes off the wall by the stairs. I was watching for the shadows which would signal their return. I don't think I was really able to connect the man and woman who had so violently abused me with my own father and the woman he had ordered me to call Mum.

They must have heard me moaning in terror when eventually I saw the shadows I feared reappearing and the dreaded figures came back into view. They came down the stairs towards me and simply carried on where they had left off. It was the beginning of an agony I was to endure for many years to come.

This time, when they had finished their horrible acts they released me and sent me back upstairs. They didn't help me as I struggled towards the daylight, barely able to walk. In fact Rose laughed at my predicament. She seemed to find the whole thing incredibly funny. I made it to the bathroom and tried to clean myself up. I had blood all over me and I hurt so much. I froze when Rose pushed her way in, fearing another onslaught, but instead she gave me a sanitary towel to put into my underwear. I was sobbing quietly as I tried to get rid of the evidence of their assault. She looked at me as if I were making a huge fuss about nothing.

'I'm sorry,' she said, obviously not meaning it. 'Everybody does it to every girl. It's a father's job. Don't worry, and don't say anything to anybody. It's something everybody does but nobody talks about.'

The thought went through my mind at that moment that nobody would want to talk about what I had just been through. It was no wonder they kept their mouths shut.

* * *

Out of the Shadows

The contraption that Fred and Rose used to rape me and destroy my virginity was one of my father's little inventions. He made many of them and over the years I was the guinea pig forced to wear them, much to the amusement of my parents and to my own never-ending humiliation. The object they used that day was something I was forced to wear regularly as time went on. At the time he first used it on me it was really just a large vibrator placed in a metal cylinder, but later he refined it into a portable version with a sort of belt made from a piece of metal which was extended into a cylindrical shape. The vibrator was placed inside the cylinder and the victim had to wear the contraption round her waist with the vibrator inserted inside her.

For some years I was forced to walk around the house doing the dusting and other jobs while wearing this, switched on, and barely covered by a little mini-skirt. Rose would get a real kick out of it and if Dad came home from work and found me in it he would just laugh with her.

The rape marked the end of the little-girl relationship I had with my father. Now I was constantly looking over my shoulder waiting for the next attack to come. I was wary and I never wanted to go down into the basement for anything. I found the whole thing so hard to understand. I thought my father loved me, so how could he hurt me and cause me pain? After that first rape they left me alone for a while. They gave me the impression that now Dad had done his duty it was all over. But I think the real reason was that I was so sore and damaged inside they knew they could not continue it for a while. But eventually I healed and the nightmare resumed.

8

Family Life

The things I told WDC Hazel Savage when I first talked to her had been locked inside my head for years. Since the moment they all came tumbling out at Tuffley Police Station they have refused to go back into the same compartment. Secrets trapped in a part of my brain marked 'Danger – Do Not Disturb' are now part of my everyday life. I had to dredge them up time and time again for police statements and every time I did, I relived them. I had to prepare myself, too, to reveal the most intimate and terrifying moments of my life to a courtroom full of strangers, and to be questioned and called a liar about things no one in her right mind would ever want to make up.

To write this book I have had to experience them yet again. It has brought great pain, but in some ways it has been a kind of therapy. Now that so much of it is known to other people – and perhaps it can help them to understand why I am as I am – it is a kind of release. But no amount of counselling will ever help me come to terms with the fact that the man I worshipped, my father, could inflict so much pain and humiliation on the child I once was.

The abuse continued for the rest of my childhood and well into my teenage years. I had no choice but to suffer it. I was a victim of my parents' sexual fantasies. To complain was to to increase the torture and provoke severe beatings. And in any case, there was no one to tell. The other children in the family were much younger and I was scared of the people who visited the house and appeared to share Fred's and Rose's sick pleasures. There was nobody outside the family I could call on. As I have explained, our contacts beyond the family and Cromwell Street were very limited, and although Rose was forced to send me to school I didn't go regularly and formed few relationships I could trust.

You have to remember, too, that all this first started happening to me over twenty years ago. Children then were not as informed as they are today about the rights and wrongs of the society in which they live and about where they can go for help. We didn't see much television, listen to the radio or go to the cinema on a regular basis. There were few books, magazines or newspapers around to tell me that my family was different from everybody else's. I was constantly reassured by my father and stepmother that what I was enduring was normal and I was never tempted to discuss it with other youngsters, partly because of a sense of shame which I did not truly understand and partly because I was under orders not to. What eight-year-old could rationalise such abuse and know where to go for help even today?

I carried on doing as I was told, trying to black out the nightmare. Frequently they said I deserved the pain because I was such a naughty child. I believed them and so I tried harder to please everyone. I used to look out of the window at children playing in the street, laughing and running around, and wonder how they could look so happy when they must be suffering as I was. I could only think that they were stronger characters and that my stepmother was right – I had a difficult, wimpish nature and I was inclined to whinge. These other kids obviously just got on with life, so I should try to do the same.

There was an occasion when I was about ten years old when, for no apparent reason, Rose made me have a boiling hot bath. The temperature was almost scalding and I nearly passed out. I kept begging to be allowed to get out but she wouldn't let me. When she eventually did I was as red as a lobster and hot and dizzy. Then she spent an age smothering me in baby oil. She never said why, she just did it. I suppose it was just another of her domination games. Rose just loved to be the boss.

On another peculiar day when I was roughly the same age, or a little older, Rose made me strip off all my clothes and stand naked agaisnt a blank wall. Then she took a photograph of me. I didn't want her to, but she forced me to stand there with threats of what would happen if I didn't. The police found the photograph during their investigations and showed it to me, asking if I remembered when it was taken. You could see from the picture how reluctant I was to pose. The body language is obvious. I was just developing; I had tiny little breasts and she made me show them off. I held my arms straight with my fists clenched. The police had the picture analysed by a psychologist. He said you could see how unhappy I was.

The day the photograph was taken I had just got out of the bath. Rose called me into her bedroom. She had a polaroid camera and said she wanted me to pose for a nice picture for her. She wouldn't let me put my clothes on. I remember thinking, 'My God, what is this for?' I suppose I knew it wasn't normal, but I couldn't do anything about it so I just stood there, rigid. The police have since told me that there is a similar picture of each child in the family taken at around the same age, so I guess Rose had a little collection. But it's hardly the usual family snapshot, is it?

One of my most horrific memories must have been one of Rose's favourite moments. She achieved my ultimate humiliation in front of all my siblings and my father. As usual it had sexual conotations, but to my warped stepmother it was just one big joke and yet another way of putting me firmly in my place as the unwanted member of the family. She stripped me naked and got the younger children to paint pictures on me with fingerpaints. The kids used pink ones, the kind of paints you can buy in Mothercare and little ones love making a mess with. The children were having fun and although I didn't like it, I could cope. But then Rose joined in. She made me get on all fours and, using black paint, she wrote the words 'black hole' on my bottom with a huge arrow. I had to stay like that all afternoon until Dad came home.

When he arrived she made me stand there and said to him: 'I've been doing some painting, love.'

Dad just laughed. He thought it was very funny. But me, well I just felt humiliated, totally humiliated. I tried to wash off the paint in the bath and then just sat on the floor and cried.

Rose regularly received male visitors, and even as a child I began to suspect what she was up to with them. They were always taken to another part of the house and used the separate doorbell fixed to the big iron gates at the entrance to our house. It had a different ring from the other bell and was reserved for Rose's friends, as they were termed. And look out anyone who used it by mistake!

I suppose I was about twelve when my suspicions about Rose were confirmed. It was my father who revealed her sordid secret, and he relished the chance to do it. One afternoon I was sitting in the lounge playing with the younger children when my father came in and beckoned me into the hallway. I had heard Rose's buzzer go and the front door open some minutes before but had taken no notice – it wasn't an unusual occurrence. I had no idea what my father wanted, but I obeyed instinctively and followed him out into the passage.

'Anna-Marie, I've got something I want to show you. You wait till you see this. But don't ever tell your mother I showed you. Just keep your mouth shut, all right?'

I was a bit dubious. I didn't really want to be in possession of any knowledge that could bring threats from Rose, but I dutifully followed my father upstairs nonetheless. He was grinning and trying not to laugh with the effort of being quiet as we approached Rose's own special room. I began to think this was going to be some kind of big joke, and I was giggling too.

The door to my stepmother's room had a wooden name plaque on it. My father took a small screwdriver out of his pocket and began very quietly to remove it. There were noises coming from inside the room which masked the small sounds he was making but I couldn't tell what was going on inside.

When the name plate came off the door I could see a small spyhole underneath. It was the type of thing you put on the front door to check who is there before answering. Dad put his eye to the hole and started to chuckle. Then he moved back and pushed me towards it. 'Go on, just have a look through there. Just take a look at that,' he urged.

I put my right eye to the hole and peered through. I could quite easily make out what was happening in the room. My stepmother was on the big bed with a black man. You could see everything they were doing. I gasped and drew back, shocked at the sight. I put my hand over my stomach, suddenly feeling a bit sick.

My father, his face flushed, looked at me. 'Don't you wish you were in there?' he asked.

I shook my head as he lined up again to have another good look through the peephole. I was stunned, totally stunned. I could quite believe what Rose was doing, but I was staggered by my father's excited reaction. I went back to the living room where the children were playing. My father followed me, but all he said was: 'Don't say nothing.'

I was quite happy to keep the knowledge to myself and when Rose's visitor had left and she came in to the living room I glanced away and tried not to have any eye contact with her at all. She was wearing a nightdress which she always wandered around in after having 'friends' round.

For the rest of the evening I avoided looking at Rose. I think I watched a little television with the younger children and then got them ready for bed. I didn't want to discuss what I had seen with anybody and so I was horrified, after the little ones were settled down, to find that my father had told Rose all about it. I think he was so excited by the idea of me seeing what was going on and watching it with him that he just had to tell her. Having sworn me to secrecy, he just couldn't resist letting the cat out of the bag himself. Rose was not amused. She went mad with Dad and screamed at him. She told him he shouldn't have done it, but she didn't have a go at me. I was amazed. I think it was the one and only time Rose ever stuck up for me.

Yet despite her assertion at the time that I should not have been introduced to her extra-curricular activities, it wasn't long before she became keen for me to take part in them. I was introduced to her clients mostly by nicknames, although I never knew some of them by any name at all. It was obvious from the start what was expected of me, and under the usual threats from Rose, I complied. I didn't like what was going on, and didn't give my consent, but I didn't have any choice. If I complained I got a hiding and still had to do it anyway, so it was easier to grit my teeth, do as I was told and submit.

Whenever any kind of sexual contact took place with these men Rose was always in the room. She couldn't risk me talking to them or them talking to me. For a start they had all been told I was a lot older than I was and my parents didn't want me revealing that I was barely a teenager. I was very well developed for my age, quite a big girl, but it was obvious I was very young, still a child. I was naïve, too, so it must have been obvious to all of them that Rose was lying about my age. Of course all these men later told the police they believed I was at least sixteen, but I don't imagine they actually cared at the time.

Most of Rose's clients were West Indians living in the Gloucester area. They liked her. They regularly described her as 'a good ride' and she couldn't get enough of them. She loved it all. She often said she needed West Indian men because she was big 'down below' and they were better endowed than white men and could satisfy her. Most of the men were regulars and would have sex with me and my stepmother. Sometimes I had to go first, sometimes second, but she was always there, watching. I rarely had to watch her. If she went first I had to wait outside the door until I was called in.

I can't remember too much about these men individually. I suppose it is yet another horror I have tried to blank out. But I was always grateful that in the main they were polite and none of them were violent. All they wanted was straight sex. They didn't knock me around and I didn't have to do anything out of the ordinary.

There were about five regulars and occasionally somebody new. I was never sure how old they were — when you are a child it is difficult to judge the age of adults and besides, I tried not to think about them too much when I didn't have to. Looking back, I suppose they were probably in their late twenties or early thirties, but it was hard to tell. One man reminded me of Michael Jackson because of his Afro haircut. But they were all clean and smelled of aftershave. Nevertheless, for me the whole thing was such a painful experience. They were all well-endowed men and I was just a child and not yet properly developed. Sometimes the act seemed to take hours and hours, and by the time they had finished I was so sore. But I never let Rose see how terrible it all made me feel in case she made it worse for her own sadistic pleasure.

There was one client who became quite keen on me. He didn't really want to have much to do with Rose — it was me he was coming to see. On one occasion he brought me a box of chocolates as a present. Rose took them from me and thanked him on my behalf. But later she got intense enjoyment from sitting down in front of me and scoffing the lot. That man never came back: Rose didn't want competition.

If it was prostitution, which I suppose it was, it was of a

most unusual kind, for Rose never wanted money from her clients — at least, not in those days — and I never saw her take any when I lived at Cromwell Street. Instead she asked for and accepted presents. She wasn't really doing it for financial gain, but mainly because she simply enjoyed it. She would drop hints about what she would like and the men usually brought cigarettes or drink, Bacardi rum, mostly. One man worked at a local meat-pie factory and brought pork pies all the time. The poor kids got fed up with pork pies. The damned fridge was packed with them and they had them served up every which way. We all got so fed up with them. When he brought some with egg in them it came as a welcome relief!

I was never sure where Rose found her clients. Dad did a lot of building work for the West Indian community, so I suppose he introduced her to some of them. Rose and Dad also used to drink in a local club where they all went and at the Wellington Arms, which was another favourite pub. Since all this came out there have been a lot of West Indian gentlemen in Gloucester waiting for a knock on the door. One or two went voluntarily to the police to make statements because they couldn't bear to wait any longer to see whether they would be named as visitors to Cromwell Street. Others, now in their sixties, have mysteriously decided to retire to Jamaica, where they originally came from. I feel sorry for their families: I don't suppose their wives or children had any idea what they were up to. Now, of course, some of these men are trying to cover up what went on to protect themselves. I expect they feel it all happened such a long time ago. It has caused heartache for their families, but they ought to remember the heartache it caused me all those years ago, and still does.

I don't know whether any of my sisters had to perform

with Rose's clients. Mae got herself a boyfriend when she was very young. I always felt it was a deliberate ploy to keep my father and others from abusing her. Things were different for Mae anyway, because she was Rose's own daughter, not Dad's by someone else.

I am not sure about Heather. She was certainly unhappy and sullen just before she died, and it seems from what she told her friend Denise that she too was beginning to experience the kind of abuse I had to put up with. I suppose that's why I didn't really doubt the story that she had just upped and left. After all, that's precisely what I did at about the same age.

But even if not all of us had to join in my stepmother's sordid lifestyle we certainly all knew about it, my brother Stephen, too. The police were staggered when they searched through my parents' belongings at Cromwell Street. Rose didn't hide her predilections or preferences. One of the things they found was her record book. In it she would keep detailed information about all the men she had sex with. She would mark them on a scale of 1 to 10 for performance, note the size of their penises and how good they were, what they liked and what she liked to do with them. It must have made bizarre reading for the police officers.

Another of this sick woman's souvenirs must also have taken the detectives by surprise. She had a Roses chocolates container full of men's soiled underwear. She used to write the date on them. She had another little box in which she stored the ashes of men's underwear she had burned. God knows why she did it, but it was typical of her twisted sense of humour.

9

Fred West

Before my ordeal in the cellar at Cromwell Street I never really noticed my father's crudeness, but as I got older I became more and more aware of it. As a child I gave him unreserved affection and devotion, but although a strong bond was maintained I began to feel embarrassed and ashamed and had no desire to introduce my family to schoolfriends during my early teens.

I was also becoming aware that the relationship I had with my father was not the same as other girls had with theirs. There was never a blinding flash when I saw that what was happening to me was wrong or not normal, it more of a gradual realisation that other people's lives were different. But there was still nothing I could do about it, no one I could tell and no way to evade the violent retribution which followed if I attempted to change things. It carried on for all these reasons, and also because I knew no other way of life.

My father's abuse continued without a break until I ran away from home at fifteen. From the time I was ten it was a regular thing, and I didn't object because it was the only way I knew of getting his affection. He would take me with him when he went on building jobs and I became quite useful. Even today I do all my own DIY. I built a stone chimney breast in my little council house, I do all my own decorating and even know the ancient art of dry-stone walling. Dad would introduce me with pride to his customers and joke that one day I would be taking over the business from him. I would help him mix artex and cement. People loved it; we must have looked like a wonderful father-and-daughter act. He used to do a lot of work for the local West Indian community and the elderly black ladies would take me into their kitchens and give me biscuits and tea with evaporated milk. They thought I was so cute. What they didn't know was that when they left us alone in the house, or in a different part of it, my father would have sex with me.

On other occasions he would do it in the back of the van he used to transport his tools. He would park somewhere remote on our way to or from a job. Often he gave me money afterwards, and said: 'Sorry, love, here, have some pocket money, but don't tell your mother.' I never intended to, but I pocketed the money just the same.

When my father did these things to me there was almost a sense of affection about it. He would kiss me on the mouth, which I hated. But none of it ever lasted long, and I just switched off. It was almost as if I were his girlfriend, not his daughter. But it was the only kind of love I knew from him and I never complained. I didn't mind keeping it a secret from Rose. In a way it was something I had over her, something I knew and she didn't.

My stepmother
Rose aged 6
© *South West News*

My father Fred on
his motorbike as a
teenager surrounded
by members of his
family
© *South West News*

My father Fred
(right) aged 2 and
his bother
© *South West News*

My sister Charmaine months before she vanished (left), our baby sister Heather and me aged about 6
© *South West News*

My sister Heather as a schoolgirl
© *South West News*

From my scrapbook, my half-brother Stephen, just 11 years old (left)

(far left) I was so proud to be made Form Captain

An early family photo of my father Fred, my mum Catherine, my sister Charmaine and me in the pushchair on a day-trip to Scotland

My grandparents, Walter and Daisy West

Me as a baby in my dad's ice cream van

A wedding group picture with Fred, Rose and my in-laws in the basement at Cromwell Street

Fred and Rose – the devoted couple
© *Express Newspapers*

My marriage to Chris with my dad proudly looking on

(below)
Me and my dad on my Wedding Day

Dad and I having a celebratory sherry at my wedding reception in the basement of Cromwell Street

Pictures from my family album showing my father Fred with my daughter Michelle (top) and stepmother Rose with Michelle (left)

My father Fred and stepmother Rose

Laying flowers at the spot where my mother
Catherine Costello was found buried
© *Express Newspapers*

Out of the Shadows

Pyschologists say that it is not uncommon for abused daughters to maintain an affection for their father. They could explain it better than I can, but it is true: part of me still loves my father despite what happened to me and what I know now. I can't help it – he was my dad, and that's that. It doesn't mean I approved of or condoned anything he did, just that I can't separate myself from him entirely. To me he was sick; he must have been sick to have done all those dreadful things.

Dad's crude expressions and strong language were an embarrassment to all the girls in the family. Rose, too, related everything to sex. You couldn't just have friends of the opposite sex, no matter what age you were. You had to be going at it like rabbits all the time. A good seeing-to would keep you in line; every woman needed a man, and by woman they meant every female from about eight upwards.

I remember cringing when my father looked at me and commented: 'I see Harry Rags is riding in the two-thirty.' That was his way of saying you had your period. We always wondered how he knew, but he did. And if any of the girls were a bit irritable around that time, he would say: 'You need a man to knock that out of you.' The implication was always that he was the man to do it. When I was about fourteen I had my first real boyfriend. He was in my year at school, and was just a pal to start with. Dad's furious and scathing reaction was typical. 'You want a real man, not a kid,' he told me. It was hardly the way most fathers would sum up their daughter's first schoolgirl crush, and there was more than a little distorted jealousy in his anger.

Apart from the sexual abuse, my father was rarely violent towards me. He left that to Rose. But he was quite capable of black rages and then his violence, because it was unusual, was all the more shocking. He and Rose often used to have a bit of a go at each other and Fred was not beyond deliberately goading her into a fury just to sit back and enjoy the show. However, there was one day when my father unleashed a temper I had barely known existed — and I was the butt of it. I was about fourteen years old when he gave me a beating equal to any of Rose's best.

Dad had gone to work early, as he always did. For some reason, Rose seemed to be dreading his return. She was very, very frightened but she wouldn't tell me why. She just kept pacing around the house, looking anxious and smoking. She begged me not to go to school but would give me no reason why I shouldn't. In the end I did as she asked and stayed at home. As the day wore on she became more and more jumpy as the clock ticked towards four o'clock, when Dad was due home from work. The moment he walked through the door he started on at my stepmother. He was having a real go at her but I couldn't work out what it was about. It seemed to me to be the only time Rose had ever needed me, and foolishly, I intervened. 'Oh come on, Dad, leave Mum alone.'

He turned on me in an instant. 'Who do you think you fucking are, acting all bloody high and mighty?' He grabbed hold of my head and thumped me hard. I fell to the floor as he continued to lay into me. Then, with almighty force, he kicked me in the mouth with the toe of his steel-capped boots. I screamed in pain as the blood spurted everywhere. I could feel my lips swelling up and clutched at my face. I turned and looked at Rose for help, for sympathy, for anything. She was laughing at me.

'Serves you fucking right,' she said.

Through my battered mouth I mumbled: 'But I was trying to protect you . . .'

Her stare was blank as she just turned and walked away.

There was one other occasion which stands out and for which I never had an explanation. It took place about a year before the incident I have just described. Rose wanted to go out on the town but for some reason my father didn't, so I was deputised to go with her. I was about thirteen but made up to look more grown up. I don't think I looked tarty, just older and, I thought at the time, quite pretty. In those days, whenever Rose went out she always looked presentable. She would dress nicely and put on a little make-up, some blusher and maybe lipstick. And she was always clean. Mind you, she often went out without any underwear and would quite brazenly sit with her legs open.

The night we went out together, Dad dropped us off somewhere just outside Gloucester at a pub. Rose and I went in and he drove off. She bought me a glass of barley wine.

'I don't like this stuff. It tastes horrible,' I told her.

'Don't moan, just fucking drink it. We're having a good time and I don't want you ruining it.'

She bought me a packet of crisps to shut me up and as usual I obeyed her and drank the barley wine. I drank the next one and the one after that, too. Men were buying us drinks and Rose seemed to be enjoying herself. She rarely bought her own drinks, there always seemed to be someone willing to treat her.

The rest of the evening is a bit of a blur. I was feeling quite drunk and rather ill. Rose took one look at me and said: 'Come on, then. We're going.' We started to walk home down a country lane. It was quite late and pretty dark. Suddenly, Dad's van appeared and Rose's whole demeanour changed. She became really evil. She grabbed hold of me and chucked me into the back of the van. 'Do you think you could be my fucking friend? Who do you think you are?'

She gave me a real hiding, just laid into me, unprovoked. Dad pulled the van over somewhere and I thought, 'Thank God, he's going to stop her.' But he just got in the back of the van and joined in. They beat me repeatedly and then the pair of them sexually abused me. When it was over they just drove home to Cromwell Street, where the rest of the children had been left unattended.

As usual I made my way painfully to the bathroom, washed my injuries and crawled into bed. I blotted out the pain and pulled down the mental barriers. I didn't even wonder why they had done it.

I am sure that during all this time my father and Rose were still having a sexual relationship. In later years, after I had left home, he would join in when she had her clients there, but mainly as a voyeur, to watch or film the proceedings. If Rose had persuaded another woman into bed with her, Fred would be all for a threesome.

Fred and Rose did sleep together. They had a bedroom which they shared but Rose also had her own room, where she entertained her clients, which she kept especially nice and was hers alone. You didn't go in unless you were invited. Things changed a bit after the older children left and they began to take in fewer lodgers. Then Dad converted the top floor of the house into a separate flat which Rose used for her entertaining and where he shot the pornographic films of her performances. Rose often used to tell people she was just a lodger at the house. She also had some other premises, in Stroud Road in Gloucester, where she worked under the name of Mandy Rose and did a lot of business.

Rose was certainly running her operation in a more professional manner than she had done in the old days. Now it wasn't just for sheer enjoyment but more for the money. Although, knowing her, I doubt that she ever stopped enjoying her perversions; if anything they got worse, and I don't think she could live without them.

As for Fred, despite the fact that he could get whatever he wanted at home, whether from his wife or his daughter, it wasn't enough for him, either. I was often aware as a child that dad was having affairs with other women. Sometimes they were women who came to the house; sometimes, like Shirley Robinson, they were lodgers. It would have been very difficult for him to hide his relationship with Shirley. She was pregnant and not far off giving birth when she went missing, and everyone was aware that Fred was the father. He used to put his arm around her and say, 'This is my next wife.' Rose's eyes would narrow, but she never said much about it.

There was another woman Fred got pregnant. I don't feel I should name her because she and her son moved right away from Gloucester some years ago and now have their own lives. The police have been in touch with them and I have written to them. The boy is, of course, my half-brother. His name is Stephen, the same name as one of my other brothers has. His mother had a fixation on my dad – he could be very charming. She desperately wanted a baby and she had one with Dad, but to him she was just another woman he conned.

Stephen, who is about two years younger than me, went to the same school as I did and I remember him quite well. I don't know how I knew he was my brother, I just did. He was a very unhappy little boy who hated being away from his mum and I used to look after him. He is dyslexic and had terrible problems with his school work. Quite often the teachers would call me out of my class and send me to calm him down because he had got upset about something and become destructive. I would just put my arm around him and say, 'Come on, it's OK, I'll help you.' Sometimes the only way they could deal with him was to call me. He would cling to me and I would comfort him.

When he was about eight, Stephen came to stay with us at Cromwell Street for a while. His mum, who was Scottish, had to go into hospital for an operation and then needed time to recuperate. In the evenings at home I would try to teach him to read and write properly, but it was difficult for him. We became very close and I think he relied on me. When his mum wanted him back Fred and Rose decided for some reason that they wanted him to stay and refused to hand him over.

Stephen made a statement to the police about an incident which happened at that time. It shows once again the terrifying violence Rose could unleash at a moment's notice.

I can see us now, two kids left in the house on our own and me looking for things to use for a reading lesson for my half-brother. On a shelf in the lounge I found an envelope. Perhaps I was intentionally rummaging around to see what I could find. Anyway, I discovered an envelope addressed to Stephen. 'Hey, look at this. It's a card, and it's for you,' I said excitedly.

He looked doubtful. 'It can't be. I can't read, so why would anyone write to me?'

'It *is* for you,' I said, opening the envelope and instinctively casting a quick look over my shoulder for trouble. I carefully took out the card and found a letter folded inside it. 'It's from your mum.'

His eyes lit up and we settled down on the floor so I could

read it to him. I don't think it occurred to either of us that if Fred and Rose had wanted him to see the letter they would have given it to him. We were just excited about our discovery. I hadn't got more than a few lines through the letter when Rose came in. We had been so intent on what we were doing that we hadn't heard her coming. I stopped reading at once but it was too late to hide the card or the letter. My heart was in my mouth and Stephen looked nervous and began to cry. We both knew what was coming next.

Rose launched herself at us and neither of us was quick enough to get away. We were still on the floor and easy targets as her fists and feet failed. Stephen probably came off the worst. She ground her Stiletto heel into his face and just missed his eye. To this day he still has a scar there.

Stephen's account of that incident formed one of the early charges against Rose, an assault on an eight-year-old boy. When the police interviewed him he said he remembered me and mentioned how kind I had been to him. I was really pleased to hear that. I am glad that someone who lived through that period of my life thinks well of me. I wrote to him and said so. I would have liked to have gone straight to see him, but it's difficult to know what to say in such circumstances.

Stephen eventually got away from Cromwell Street. Fred and Rose kept refusing to hand him over so one day, when they were out, she turned up, got into the house somehow and simply took him. They were furious, but they couldn't do anything about it. I think she left Gloucester straight away in case they came after her. I thought about him sometimes and wondered how he was getting on, but of course he was not the only person to have vanished from my life overnight and in time my memories of him faded. Thankfully, for him at least, the parting meant the start of a better life.

10

Rose West

Rose would have made a wonderful concentration camp guard. She exhibited an evil unknown since the days of the Nazis as far as I was concerned. She would have enjoyed wielding her power over the poor inmates of those terrible places. Torture, both mental and physical, would have been her forte. Nothing would have pleased Rose more than to send so many to their deaths and to have unlimited scope to experiment on them and torture them before they went. But she was born in a different time and in a different country so instead 25 Cromwell Street became the territory behind the wire and the family, unsuspecting lodgers and serveral unfortunate young women snatched from the streets, the victims.

My stepmother would inflict pain with either a detached indifference or a calculated and controlled excitement. She seemed to feel little pain herself and could shrug off any physical retaliation with ease. Being beaten up by Rose was like going ten rounds with Frank Bruno, but without the laughs later. To watch her go into one of her major rages was like watching a horror movie. Her expression would change: you would see a coolness transforming her face. It would go like porcelain, very cold and translucent. Then her eyes would disconnect. When she got really angry and began to hit you, she would froth at the mouth and spit. She was like a wild dog. Evil, truly evil.

If Cromwell Street was my prison when I was growing up, then Rose was my jailer. It was almost impossible to get out of the house without her permission. Internal and external doors were often locked, as were the huge iron gates which led to the street. Even Rose's own bedroom door was almost always locked and she wore the key to it on a chain round her neck. She often had the keys to other rooms and doors with it, either on the same chain or on a big ring clipped to a belt round her waist.

She like to wear a big, thick, black leather belt under her clothes. At one time she even had a weightlifter's belt and you could see that she enjoyed wearing it. It made her look butch and powerful. The belts served a dual purpose. They could be unbuckled in a flash and used as a weapon or they could be fastened tight around a victim's arms or hands so he couldn't escape.

If she was going to use the belt to give you a thrashing, Rose would wet it first. Damp leather stings, and she liked to inflict as much pain as possible. She would use both ends of the belt. Once she lashed me between the legs with the buckle end and I was bruised and bleeding by the time she had finished.

I realise now that I was the guinea pig on whom they perfected the techniques they used to torture and kill some of those poor young women. They experimented on me to see what methods could be used to restrain their victims and what would hurt and make them suffer most, and I know only too well what must have happened to them. I cannot say how many times I was abused by Fred and Rose, together or individually. The countless separate incidents have now blurred into one ghastly nightmare. But I will never forget the methods they used.

They frequently practised forms of restraint on me. It was usually Rose who did the tying-up. Sometimes I would be tied with my hands behind my back, sometimes tightly in front of me or with some loose rope between them. I might be secured to the bed with my legs spreadeagled or bound together. It was trial and error; she seemed to be trying to establish which way caused the most pain as well as which was the most successful at limiting my movements.

The materials varied too. Sometimes she ripped old sheets into strips and used them to tie my arms or legs or to stop me yelling out. Rose liked to pull the sheet really tight across your mouth, almost like a bridle on a horse. When she had finished with them she would recycle them for dusters. She got a kick out of builders' rope, or nylon clothesline, tied so tight your limbs went numb. On other occasions, she used carpet tape to bind my arms and legs and fabric to put across my mouth. It was thick and black and had a kind of fabric backing to it. She never used so much that she had to cut it off – she simply ripped at it viciously when she had finished with you. Once she tried that white plastic they use on parcels, and that really hurt.

Once I was trussed up and unable to move the assault would begin. Rose had a variety of weapons she loved to start off with. Apart from the belts, she had canes and whips, including a cat-o'-nine-tails. She didn't seem to have a favourite; she might use just one of them or a selection. When she had completed her experiments she would encourage Dad to rape me or they would both insert objects into me.

By the time I was old enough to start dealing with Rose's clients I no longer needed to be tied to the bed. It wasn't that I was willing – just too scared to disobey. Fear was enough to keep me under Rose's and Fred's control, but nevertheless they may have used other means too.

One morning when I was about fourteen, probably not too long before I ran away, Rose offered to make my breakfast. I was staggered – normally you got your own, were quick about it and tried not to be noticed while you ate it. But today she handed me a bowl of Weetabix mashed up with hot milk. I mumbled a confused thank you, sat at the kitchen table and began to eat. I was about halfway through when I realised I was munching on something hard and chalky. I was too scared to spit it out, but I moved my spoon around in the bowl to see if I could identify it. Rose sat opposite me watching my every move. I put another spoonful into my mouth and began to retch, spitting part of it back into the bowl. 'Ugh. there's something in it. It's horrible.'

She reached over the table and clipped me across the head. 'It's only a piece of grain. Put it in your mouth and eat it.' Her voice was steely and brooked no argument.

My head lowered and my eyes downcast, I carried on eating, unable to avoid the partly crushed white tablets I could now make out in my cereal.

Years later a witness whom the court called Miss A in order to protect her identity told the police she had been tied up, raped and beaten by Rose and Fred at Cromwell Street, a horrifying story to which I shall return later. The

Out of the Shadows

attack was observed by a teenage girl who was naked and sitting on the floor, just watching. She didn't appear to be uncomfortable or surprised by what was happening and may have been high on something. The appalling degrading acts which took place in that room that day shocked everyone who heard or read Miss A's evidence. The description of the watching girl matched me in every respect, but I have no memory of the incident — not even a glimmer of something long forgotten or blocked out. Yet there can be little doubt I was there.

My father enjoyed sparking off some of Rose's most memorable furies. He came home from work one evening and found her in the kitchen stirring something on the cooker. I was laying the table ready for supper and some of the other children were around the house. Dad went up behind her and mumbled a few things in her ear. Then he began poking her with his finger and jumping back out of the way. She turned and gave him a sour look. He did it again and again. 'Come on then, come on. What's up Rose, eh? Come on.' The more he poked her in the arm or back, the quieter and stiffer she became. Once she said: 'Watch it, boy, just watch it or I'll fucking have you.' But he didn't. He just kept right on.

I kept my head down and got on with my task, but every now and then I cast a glance upwards to see what would happen next. The tension was building but I didn't want to say anything in case they transferred their interest to me. Dad was laughing and as well as prodding my stepmother he was punching her now, not hard, but none too gently, either. He seemed to think it was a big game but I felt the knot in my stomach grow. I wanted desperately to leave the room but I didn't want to make any movement in case it reminded them that I was there. All of a sudden, Rose half turned from the cooker. She snapped: 'I fucking warned you, fella.' Dad gave her one more prod and she swung round and snatched up the carving knife from the work surface. Some of the younger children had come into the kitchen and they went one way as I went the other. My father made a dash for it and she ran after him with the carving knife flashing in her hand. Dad ran to the back patio doors, through the archway and up towards the steps to the old living room, which was a bedroom at the time.

He got to the top of the stairs and slammed the door shut. Rose lifted the knife and stabbed at the closed door. So fierce was the blow that the knife stuck halfway through the solid wood door, but not before it had nearly taken off the fingers of Rose's right hand. She didn't say a word. She calmly went back into the kitchen, picked up a tea towel and wrapped it around her hand. Dad followed her and was looking at the bloody wound. Rose said to him: 'Right, fella. You've got to take me down the hospital.' She didn't cry. Her fingers were literally hanging off by the tendons and the skin, but there was simply no reaction. At the hospital they had to sew all the tendons back together and even today Rose can only partly close her hand.

She came home from hospital the next day with her arm in plaster. They told her to go back for a check-up and to have the stitches out, but she didn't bother. It used to itch and would poke a big knitting needle inside the plaster to scratch it. When she got fed up with it Dad used some big carpet scissors to cut off the plaster and Rose took out the stitches herself.

As I said before, although much of Rose's violence was directed at me I didn't have a monopoly on it. Even the younger children got more than their fair share. When they were very tiny she didn't tie them up, she just pinned them down and beat the hell out of them. She knew that as long as the marks didn't show she could do anything she wanted. And if there was visible evidence of a beating she just kept them home from school.

My brother Stephen, Rose's son by Dad, spoke up for his mother and defended her when she was first arrested. I can't think why, because he suffered at her hands just like everyone else. Once when he was just a little boy he clashed with her over his breakfast. All children have likes and dislikes, but they weren't allowed in our house. I was big as a teenager because I would eat whatever the other children didn't like, even if I hated it myself, just so it wouldn't be left on their plates and used as an excuse for a beating. Mae hated any meat with fat on it. Rose knew this and always dished up the fattiest bit she could find for Mae. I would spear it from her plate and eat it when no one was looking.

Stephen was not keen on fried eggs. One morning he ended up with one and pushed it around his plate until his mother noticed he wasn't eating it. 'Eat that egg, boy.' Rose and Dad always called Stephen 'boy'. It used to remind me of the character in *Tarzan*.

Stephen looked mutinous but he had enough sense to cut off a piece of the white and at least look as if he were going to do as he was told. When Rose's back was turned he chucked it quickly into the brown swing bin near the kitchen table. Unfortunately for him, before we had all left the table his mum went to throw something in the same bin. She turned and stared at him with her lip curled. 'Eat that egg, did you, boy?'

He nodded but said nothing. His eyes were wide with fear

and we all held our breath, pretty sure of what would come next. But to our surprise, instead of picking up the nearest weapon Rose opened the bin and fished out the fried egg. By now it was now covered in cigarette ash and other slime. She slapped it back down on his plate. 'Mess with me, would you, boy? Eat it.'

He had to obey. She just stood there watching him, then walked away with a manic laugh.

As the first boy in the family, Stephen got away with a lot more than the rest of us, but even so he often went too far and suffered for it. When he was about eleven or twelve he used to steal the dirty magazines from home and sell them at school. And he would pinch money from his mum's purse to buy cigarettes.

One day she discovered that he had nicked something from her room. It was either money or a cassette-player, I forget which. She telephoned the school and asked for him to be sent home. No sooner had he come through the door than she made him strip off his clothes and go into the bathroom. She used a belt to tie him, stomach down, to the lid of the toilet seat and gave him a real hiding with a big stick. Afterwards he had bruises and huge red welts all up his legs and over his bottom.

Eventually, when he was sixteen she threw Stephen out and told him to get on with it and make his own way in the world.

It was difficult to avoid it if Rose decided she was going to give you a beating, because often she would catch you unawares. It wasn't always for something you had just done; it might be for something you had done some time ago or simply because she felt like it. If you upset her and she didn't immediately retaliate it was often worse.

Out of the Shadows

You would be left wondering when you were going to get it. Rose could wait; it was psychological warfare and very unnerving. Once you realised you were in for it it was hard to get away. Often she had stripped you naked in an instant and there was nowhere to run.

I can recall tearing naked out of the bathroom, screaming, and heading for the main gates. They were locked and I couldn't get out. I ended up in a heap in the washroom, crying. But there was no one to hear, let alone to help.

Usually we didn't know what it was that brought on one of my stepmother's moods, but occasionally it was clear that it had come about as a direct result of something Dad had done. If he had a shout at her or told her to do something she didn't want to do, she would take it out on us. It was her way of getting back at Dad. If she really wanted to prove a point she made sure I was the one who suffered. She felt I was his favourite, and perhaps to some extent I was, but as I have explained, he rarely stuck up for me or told her to pack it in. When Rose had dished out a real beating or I had pleased her in some way with her 'friends' she might buy me something, a lipstick or some powder or clothes. I felt I had been given the crown jewels. I didn't connect the behaviour and the reward then, but the presents usually came about two or three days afterwards. Otherwise it was rare for me to get new clothes – mostly I wore Rose's cast-offs.

I hated the huge flowered print dresses she gave me but I had no choice but to wear them. I never looked smart, but at least I was clean. The whole family was; it was something Rose insisted on. I hated having a bath because, as I said earlier, you couldn't lock the bathroom door. Obviously, you were at your most vulnerable then, and that would be the time when Rose caught you.

I'll never forget scrambling out of the bath, enveloping my twelve-year-old, but quickly developing body in a big bath towel and trying to sneak into my bedroom and into my clothes. I had dropped the towel and grabbed at one of the hated dresses, desperate to cover myself, when Rose appeared in the dooway. She stared at me. She looked calculating. She reached forward and snatched at the dress. 'No. Forget about bloody putting that on. Get in my room.'

I thought: 'Oh God, what is going to happen now?' I said nothing but my expression gave me away.

Rose smirked. 'Look at you, you miserable cow. What's the matter, then? Don't you want it?' Her voice was almost teasing, but it had the customary hard edge. She went into her special room and I followed meekly.

'Come on, then. Come in, you silly little bitch. Get on the bed,' she ordered me.

I turned off and tuned out and prepared for another ordeal. I got on to the bed, saying nothing, and waited while she stared at me. Then she got on to the bed too and began touching herself and touching my breasts. She got angry when I wouldn't respond and, fearful of the violence I would provoke if I didn't, I showed I was willing and did as I was told. She forced me to give her oral sex and I will never forget the grossness of it as long as I live. She kept urging me: 'Come on, do it properly.' And then, 'Use your fingers.' It was absolutely horrendous. And all the time it was happening she was squeezing and scratching my breasts. She had long fingers and quite long nails, and she scratched me until I bled. She grabbed the skin at the base of my throat and twisted it until I could barely breathe.

That was Rose for you. Sex on demand — at any time, any place and with anybody she could get her hands on. If she wanted it at that moment, she got it. It didn't matter if it was Dad, one of her so-called friends, a woman or a child.

The only holiday I can remember in my childhood ended because of that woman's enormous sexual appetite. It was the very hot summer of 1976. Rose took me, some of the little ones, and her father, William Letts, to a holiday camp at Westwood Ho! in Devon. Dad didn't come because he was too busy working. I can remember getting quite bad sunburn and winning the Miss Princess of Devon competition. I was thrilled. It meant I could take part in the parade at the end of the week. But what might have been a rare happy childhood memory was thwarted. Rose's father got so angry at her behaviour that he demanded we all went home early. He was so embarrassed that he felt he just couldn't stay. Rose, in her usual fashion, had worked her way through the orchestra like a dose of salts. She was having it away night after night, either in her chalet or in theirs, and it was becoming the joke of the camp. There was an almighty row between Rose and her father and the result was that we packed our bags and I never had the chance to complete my duties as Devon Princess. The band, meanwhile, played on without us.

II

My School Years

I was never really happy at school. I felt I didn't fit in. Even at infants' and junior school I found it difficult to make friends. My home life made me reserved and I was never allowed to invite other girls and boys home or to go to their houses to play. In later years, at secondary school, my inner anger and frustration emerged as an aggressive if not delinquent streak which was not understood by those in authority or by the few friends I did have.

My school reports from my teenage years contained definite pointers to the problem but no one saw through the tough façade I maintained or bothered to probe further. Teachers then were not as aware as they are today of the behavioural signals from victims of child abuse, but even so it amazes me some kind of investigation was never made into my background. There were occasions when I was so unruly that one teacher even used to lock me in a cupboard until I calmed down. I never held this against him because he was one of the few I liked. He did it for my own good so that I wouldn't get into even more trouble with the headmaster. To my knowledge my behaviour was not even reported to my parents. I feel sure if it had been I would have received a beating for drawing attention to myself.

My home life was often mirrored in my school life. After Dad and Rose were arrested I found some of my old school reports and looked through them. They reminded me of how hard I had tried to fit in with the other children and to please and impress my teachers. These days, with the additional training teachers have, I would hope someone would pick up the signs and realise that there was something wrong. Reading the reports now it's easy to see that they scream 'abused child' — it's all there. Even then it should have registered with someone that Anna-Marie West was an unhappy girl growing into a difficult young woman. Did no one wonder why?

The earliest report I uncovered, dated 1973, when I was aged eight years, eleven months, was one from St Paul's Primary School in New Street, Gloucester. The pale green cardboard cover shows the school crest drawn in black together with my name, address and date of birth. Inside are three forms filled in by my year teacher and headmaster. The fourth one is blank, presumably because I left to go on to the juniors that year. The report isn't bad. My marks were all Cs except for English, in which I had a B–. There were forty kids in my age group and I was about halfway down in ability. Considering what happened to me at home when I was eight, I was surprised to see that my form teacher had written: 'A good year's work. She has worked hard throughout the year. She has been a very helpful member of the class.'

By the following year it was obvious that things were

slipping, I was still at about the same position in the class but now there were no Bs. Instead Ds and Es were creeping in. My new teacher summed it up: 'Anna often doesn't give herself enough time to present thoughtful work. Her presentation is very messy. Her work is often affected by her moods.' Next to the category marked 'Conduct' she wrote: 'Anna worries too much about the welfare of those around her.'

The following year was my last at St Paul's and I was preparing to go to secondary school. My headmaster, Mr Martin, described my report as 'quite satisfactory' but the new form teacher had once again noted my behaviour pattern. My marks were a mixture of Cs and Ds and I was still midway down the class. Comments on individual subjects ranged from 'Can do well when she tries' to 'Very interesting when she puts her mind to it'. The general remarks section said more. 'I think Anna has had quite a good year. Often her work has been quite good, but her moods have not helped her.' If only those well-meaning teachers had ever stopped to consider what was causing those wild mood swings.

I don't have the report which followed my first year at Linden's Secondary School, which is a shame — I tried so hard to make a new start that year. Despite what was happening at home — by them I had been introduced to Rose's clients — I kept battling on at school. The grades at Linden were applied separately for achievement and effort. Even when I didn't achieve much, my efforts earned As and Bs. But a giveaway sign was my attendance record: I was given a D for below average and the art teacher awarded me a B — for effort but commented: 'Recent absences have also hindered progress.' Mr Kidley, the maths teacher, picked up something some of the others had missed: 'Works well when she is in the mood,' he wrote.

By the time I was in the third form it was clear from my report that I was having difficulty in some subjects. Ironically, biology was not one of them. I apparently showed great interest in those classes and got my first-ever A for achievement. But other teachers noted that I was struggling despite my obvious abilities. My year tutor recorded that I had been absent on fifty-two occasions and late fifteen times. No one, it seemed, wondered why.

The last report I have is dated 1979, when I was in the fourth form. I had been absent that year sixty-eight times. It described my conduct as satisfactory; previously it had never been less than good. I'm surprised at this because I was a bit of a bully in the playground and often threw tantrums in class. I have a feeling that perhaps I was given the benefit of the doubt because some of those in authority suspected that things weren't quite right in the West household but didn't want to get involved. After all, I was due to leave the following year.

Only once did anyone become suspicious about my family circumstances and that was when I was in junior school. The PE teacher at St Paul's became anxious when yet again I brought in a note saying I could not take part in the games lesson. She insisted I could and I was adamant that I couldn't. Then she noticed the big black bruises on my legs – the real reason why I was refusing and why Rose had written to have me excused. The teacher, a jolly woman in her thirties with a kind manner, made me roll down my socks and hitch up my skirt. She gave a slight gasp as she took in the injuries. She frowned and gave me an uncertain look. 'How did you do this, Anna-Marie? Did you have an accident or did someone do it to you?'

I desperately wanted to say: 'My mum did it. She's always

doing it.' But I couldn't quite find the words. My mouth opened and shut a few times as I tried to tell her, but my fear of Rose was too great. Instead I put my head down and simply looked sullen.

'Anna-Marie. If someone did this to you, you should tell me. Now, what happened?'

She wasn't unkind. She just didn't know how to deal with the evidence of her own eyes and I wasn't about to help. I continued to look sulky and said eventually: 'I fell over, Miss. I just fell over.'

The PE teacher let me sit out the lesson and nothing more was said. The school day continued as normal and I assumed that was the end of it. But no sooner had I got back home to Cromwell Street that afternoon than the doorbell rang. Rose answered it while I was still in the hallway. The smartly dressed woman introduced herself as being from the Welfare Department. She said she wanted to talk to Mrs West because they were concerned about me. My blood ran cold but Rose kept her cool, invited the woman in and sent me to my room to change. I did as I was told and sat on the edge of my bed, trembling and biting my lip nervously. I wanted to listen in to the conversation but I was too scared to try. When I thought I had been gone long enough I headed towards the kitchen. The welfare woman was just leaving. I heard her say: 'Oh well, that's fine, Mrs West.' And she went out of the front door quite reassured and never came back again. Rose had told her a plausible enough tale about me falling downstairs and she didn't even question me on its authenticity. Not that I would have disagreed in front of Rose, of course, or at all for that matter.

Once the woman had gone I received one of the worst beatings of my life. It taught me a lesson about the welfare and those in authority – they couldn't help, and any attempts they made to do so merely rebounded on me.

Going to school got me out of the house so I rarely played truant. The absences occurred when Rose forced me to stay away for some reason of her own. My attendance record wasn't good because she would often invent an excuse to keep me at home. There were always the younger children to look after and housework to be done, or perhaps she had miscalculated and some of my bruises showed. Sometimes I was fit enough to do sport: I remember briefly being in the relay team and I have a swimming certificate. She must have been careful not to do anything that would show until after my school swimming course finished.

But there weren't really any lessons I particularly liked. Usually I preferred to wander off on my own at break time and get some peace. One of the schools I went to had a little garden with a small pond. I used to sit there and enjoy the surroundings and being away from Cromwell Street. I did try hard at school at the beginning; I would have a go at things, but there was always this suppressed feeling inside me. Even though I tried I got so frustrated. Much of this was because I never received praise for anything I did achieve. Eventually it didn't seem worth the effort. I grew disheartened; nobody was going to appreciate anything I did. We had sports days and things like that, but Fred never came and Rose turned up only very occasionally. I wouldn't dream now of missing anything my children were involved in. I know how important those things are to kids.

After junior school days I went to Linden's Secondary School in Gloucester, a brisk fifteen-minute walk from Cromwell Street, through the park and along Aston Street. It's not there now. There's just an empty space. I never took much notice of the changing seasons as I crossed the park — I didn't have time. My family knew what time school finished and exactly how long it took to get home, and if I wasn't in that door bang on 4.15 p.m. they wanted to know why. I think I was quite keen to go to Linden's. It was the big school and a bit of a fresh start, and the more Rose didn't want me to go, the more I wanted to. But of course she spoiled it for me. She went out and bought me the complete uniform from the local Co-op but she got me a blazer with the school badge on it like the boys wore and she had my hair cut so short that I looked like a boy, a real short-back-and-sides. She bought me a briefcase too. It was big and brown with a handle, like the kind of bag doctors carry. I was the only one in the school who had a briefcase. Everyone else had a proper satchel. I used to keep my books, pens and pencils in it as well as my cigarettes, a packet of ten No. 6 — I had been rolling fags for my dad from the age of nine and smoking since I was eleven.

Linden's seemed huge after junior school. There were so many children and it was frightening and intimidating. Of course the other kids used to tease me a lot. I still hadn't completely lost my Scots accent and they used to call me the Flying Scotsman. But despite the ribbing I was popular to begin with and made a good start. The children had to elect their own form captain and they chose me from four nominated first-formers. I was thrilled and so proud. It meant I had responsibilities: I had to get the right books out, sort out problems, run errands. I was somebody people could depend and rely on. I had a badge which said 'Form Captain' on it — I've still got it.

The day I was elected I rushed home to tell Dad and Rose. I had the badge pinned to my blazer and I was bursting with pride. Dad said something vague but he didn't seem to share my joy; Rose just wasn't interested. I was deflated. I was still proud of my role in class, but after that year my school life went downhill.

I had a lot of problems finding my feet. I didn't say much, I was an introvert and by the time I got to my teens I felt under extreme pressure and couldn't cope with the stress. It was difficult trying to be two people. In school I was a child, attempting to make friends, learn and pay attention in lessons, and at home there were the men and the beatings. I started to realise that other children had a different sort of life. They went to discos and parties and to their friends' homes. I listened to the other girls giggling about boys and sex in the toilets but I kept my mouth shut when they came out with ridiculous old wives' tales. Inside I was thinking: 'That's rubbish. I know how you do it and what happens,' but I never said anything. I just turned away and stayed silent.

In spite of my problems I made a few pals. There was Karen, Helen and Mark and a couple of other kids who lived at the back of Cromwell Street, around St Michael's Square and Parliament Street. But knowing them began show me the difference in our lives. They would be out at night playing in the street and I would be in the washroom at the back of the house doing the family's laundry. I could hear them playing and I would sneak out of the washroom and talk to them over the fence. If Rose caught me she would be furious, and to my embarrassment she would drag me back into the washroom and knock hell out of me with all the other kids watching. The next day they would laugh and say to me: 'Oh, you got a bit of a beating, didn't you?'

Yet I never asked those other children how things were in their households. I just accepted that what I had was what

Out of the Shadows

I had. I never had the urge to explore the subject further — I was much too frightened of my family and the consequences. Sometimes two of the girls who lived nearby, Karen and Helen, would come with me after school to where my dad was working, close to Linden's, and he would give all three of us a lift home in his van. But I was never allowed to invite the girls in. Dad would drop them off at the end of the road and remind me: 'Don't tell your mum.'

There was one memorable occasion when I was allowed to go to a party. Why the decision was made or who made it I can't recall — the details must have been overtaken by the sheer thrill of suddenly being allowed to enjoy something other teenagers took for granted. I had been invited by a girl called Sian to her birthday party at her house. I took a present and a card like all the other guests and I bought a new dress for the occasion — well, it wasn't really new, but I chose it myself from the Oxfam shop and paid for it out of the little bit of pocket money Dad slipped me for favours. It was the most beautiful dress I had ever owned and although strictly speaking it was somebody else's cast-off at least it wasn't Rose's. It was red with white spots on it and I thought it was made of silk. It probably wasn't, but it felt like silk to me. It was long, sort of calf-length, and there were masses of material in the skirt. It had short sleeves and a dip in the neckline which gave me a cleavage. It made me look much older and I felt so special. I put on a little bit of make-up and did my hair and wore a pair of brown suede high-heeled shoes, also from Oxfam.

I loved those shoes, but Rose hated them because they were really high. I wore them until there was nothing left of them. It's funny, but although I remember every tiny detail of what I wore and what I looked like that night, the party itself is just a vague blur. I don't even remember if it lived up to expectations, but I don't think it mattered anyway. The only thing that concerned me was that I fitted in with the others and looked right, and I did.

But it was no good pretending that I was the same as those other girls who spent their lives making friends, going to parties and enjoying a busy social life with the blessing of their parents. They might bitch and moan about what their mums and dads would or wouldn't let them do, but mostly they didn't mean it. They were able to sound off in the way rebellious teenagers do, safe in the knowledge that they were loved and could love in return. For me it was different. I still yearned for affection from my father and tried to please Rose. The copious reserves of love I had I lavished on my brothers and sisters. But even their responses were governed by fear of Rose. The only physical closeness I had was my father's constant abuse of me, the furtive and shameful attacks when Rose wasn't present, which I longed to resist.

When I was fifteen the inevitable occurred. My father got me pregnant. I suppose in many ways it was fortunate for me that the pregnancy didn't develop properly – it was ectopic, which meant that the embryo was developing in the Fallopian tube. It was years before I found out what had been wrong with me, even that I had been expecting a baby. I thought I had simply had something wrong inside me and had had an operation. No one ever explained and it wasn't until I had my first daughter that my doctor's notes revealed the truth.

It took me two full months to tell anybody I thought there was something the matter with me. My period seemed to be going on for all that time – I did not stop bleeding – but I was too worried and ashamed to say anything. I had a dread of anyone examining my body. That might seem strange after all that had been done to me, but those experiences had taken place against my will and I did not want to submit to anything voluntarily.

Eventually, however, I told Rose and she was forced to take me to the doctor's. I sat nervously in the waiting room, desperate for a cigarette and terrified of what might happen. The longer I waited the stronger the urge was to make a run for it, but Rose insisted that now we were there we were going to see the doctor.

We went into the small, and to me forbidding, consulting room and I sat silently while Rose explained what was wrong with me. The doctor asked me a number of personal questions and I gave monosyllabic answers, my head hanging down to save my embarrassment. He told me to lie on the couch, pulled a screen across and prodded and poked at my stomach. His face was serious and stern and he said little as he examined me. I didn't hear the subsequent conversation with Rose, but the next thing I knew I was being carted off to Gloucester Hospital.

It was my father, not Rose, who came with me. We waited for a little while before a nurse took down some notes and then another doctor took a look at me. They told me nothing but consulted quietly with my father. I was taken to a ward and put into bed. Fred told me: 'The doctors think there might be something wrong inside. They are going to put you to sleep and have a little look.' He was quite kind, but he didn't stay long. He hated hospitals and I imagine he was worried about what they might find.

I lay in bed as nurses bustled back and forth, giving me a pre-med and checking my notes. Eventually I was carted off to the operating theatre. Still no one had told me what they really thought was the matter with me and I was afraid to ask. There was just the smell of antiseptic, people in green and a man in a surgical mask whose face blurred and then nothing. When I woke up I was back in the ward. I was very groggy and I ached. To the left of me was this bag on a stand and a tube which came down and was connected to my hand. I was on a drip, but I didn't know what it meant or what it was for. I put my hand down to my tummy and felt a big padding across it. I just lay there feeling sorry for myself and too ill to appeal for reassurance.

Some time later my father came in. His face was white as a sheet. He didn't say much, just that I was allright and not to worry, and that he wasn't going to stay because he hated hospitals. I think he was only there for a matter of minutes and that was it. He visited just once more in the week I was there, but not one other member of the family came. There were no cards, no grapes, no flowers. I spent the week in a vacuum, wondering what had been wrong with me and whether I would recover.

Years later, when I saw my medical records, I understood the attitude of the doctors and nurses. They had been so offhand and unfriendly. It was 1979 and what they saw in the hospital bed was a fifteen-year-old slut who had got what she had been asking for and didn't deserve any sympathy. It wasn't that they were actively unkind, just businesslike, efficient and decidedly cool.

Well versed in keeping my mouth shut and not asking questions, I didn't press them for information and accepted their manner as the norm. After all, I wasn't used to people being nice to me anyway and I didn't expect it from strangers when I didn't get it at home. Even when the dressing was taken off and I saw the twelve metal pins in my bruised flesh I didn't question them too hard. The matron told me that the operation had been 'something to do with my periods'. I was very frightened and felt so alone. At night I sobbed quietly into my snowy-white pillow, unable to decide which I hated most, the hospital or the home to which I would have to return.

12

Phil

I wasn't entirely alone during that awful time in hospital. I had one regular visitor, one friend who never let me down, not then, and not now. Throughout my desperate teenage years right up to this day there has been one person who has believed in me, one person who has been there for me. I have treated him badly in some respects; I have pushed him away even when deep down I wanted to beg him to stay. But whenever I did so, it was because of a strong conviction that his life would be better if it wasn't linked to mine. I still find it hard to comprehend why he is still around. But now, instead of trying to break the bond that exists between us, I am grateful for it and for his support.

Phil, my school sweetheart, was only fifteen-years old when he first demonstrated his loyalty and affection. As I lay in my lonely hospital bed surrounded by older women whose families paid happy smiling visits, I looked forward each day to the moment when he would appear with a shy

'Hello, Anne,' a small gift and inconsequential school gossip which would take my mind off my troubles. He dropped in every day after classes had finished, still wearing his uniform and clutching his books. He never missed a day. He would perch on the end of my bed or sit back comfortably in the high-backed chair alongside it, never failing to cheer me up.

The first time he came I was surprised but secretly overjoyed. Phil had questioned my girlfriends at school and discovered where I was. He went straight to the hospital, tracked down the ward number, and spent more than an hour in the dreary dormitory-style room. His concern was obvious from the moment he arrived. He had no idea why I was in hospital and as I didn't know the real reason myself, and was too embarrassed to offer him the little information I did have, he simply deduced that it was 'women's problems' and didn't ask me about it. We just talked and he made me laugh; the simple fact that he was there made my life more bearable. Just before I was rushed into hospital I had been in trouble at school for fighting. Unable to control my aggressive streak, I had given another girl a right going-over. She had done very little to deserve it, no more than to talk casually to Phil. I thought she was chatting him up and, feeling threatened, lashed out. It wasn't unusual to see Anna-Marie West fling the much-hated briefcase to the ground, cast off the equally loathed blazer and erupt in a frenzy of fists and kicks, but this time I went too far. The other girl's mum complained and I was on the point of being expelled when my medical problems intervened.

It was Phil who came to my rescue. A responsible prefect, much trusted and admired by the teachers, Phil went to see the headmaster and pleaded my case. He explained that he had visited me in hospital and felt my aggression had been a symptom of my illness. Due entirely, I believe, to his intervention, I was allowed back to school when I was better and was permitted to finish the final year and take my exams.

So what was such a pillar of the school doing going out with the bad girl of the fifth form? It was a common question asked by teachers and other pupils alike. We were a most unlikely combination and the subject of much speculation. I was the bully, the fighter, the sullen unco-operative youngster whom no one could fathom and he was Mr Sensible, the teacher's favourite, the lad tipped to do well. But somehow it worked. We just clicked and understood each other. Phil was my first real boyfriend, my first proper relationship. Anything or anybody who came before Phil was put up by my parents. There were the men I was ordered to go with and the men I was told to pick up so that they could go thieving with Dad or help him with building work. But there was never a friendship with someone of my own age, never a mental and affectionate bonding with someone I genuinely wanted to care for until Phil.

My father, of course, didn't approve. Phil was someone outside the family, outside his control, and someone in whom I might confide. To Fred, he represented a danger. But Fred was dismissive of him to my face and in front of Phil himself. 'Get rid of him. You don't need a boy, Anna-Marie, you need a real man. A schoolboy's no bloody good to you,' was my father's most common reaction on seeing Phil.

I can't remember the first time I saw Phil. It wasn't love at first sight thing or anything like that, he was just someone who was always around. We were in the same year at school though not in the same class. He had just moved to the area from Bristol and I knew he had a dad and a stepmother like me, so I felt we had something in common. He was friendly with some of the lads in my class so we often found ourselves in the same gang talking in the playground. He seemed sensible and straightforward but not in the least stuck up, and it would have been difficult not to like him.

Even at fourteen I was more mature in many respects than the other girls, for obvious reasons. I was big-busted, too, and the boys at school used to eye me up. But I had too much of a reputation as a toughie for them to make an approach or even tease or make fun of me. Phil was different. He was the first male who took an interest in me as a person, who wanted to hear what I had to say. He had no hidden agenda. He made me feel worthwhile, and that gave me a warm glow inside which led me to imagine that another life might be possible.

I suppose we first got together when we were both appearing in a school drama production of *Alice in Wonderland*. Phil had quite a starring role and I was cast as the narrator. It seems amazing now that Fred and Rose let me take part. After all, it meant staying late some nights at school and then visiting another school to perform as part of a competition. We all travelled to the contest by bus and Phil, knowing I was nervous, contrived to sit near me. He chatted away and put me at my ease and the whole evening went well. We were all quite euphoric coming home and the atmosphere was something I had never experienced before. I didn't know it then, but he told me later that that was the day he fell head over heels. It was different for me – all I knew was that I desperately wanted this person's friendship and respect. I feared then and have done ever since that if he ever knew the real me, what had happened to me and the way I had been forced to live, I would never have either.

His courting of me was quiet and gentle. It began with

Out of the Shadows

taking more of an interest in me and friendly chats at break time. I was embarrassed to have to decline when eventually he asked if he could walk me home after school. 'I don't walk home,' I told told him.

'You do. You go through the park. I've watched you.'

I was offhand.'Well, that's not the way you go. You live in the opposite direction.'

'That's all right. I like the park. We can chat and then I'll walk back through the park again and back to my house. It's not a problem, and in any case I want to.' He was so insistent that there was nothing for it but to tell him the truth.

'You don't understand. I don't walk home from school. I run. I have just fifteen minutes to get back. My dad and stepmother are really strict. If I'm a minute over, they go crazy.' I kept my eyes down as I told him this but then looked up quickly to see his reaction.

'OK, I'll run home with you. But we'll go very fast at the beginning so we get there quicker and then we can talk for a few minutes before you have to go in.'

So that's what we did. Every evening after school we sprinted through the park at a speed Linford Christie would be proud of and then, after we had caught our breath and stopped laughing, we would talk for a few minutes before I made the final dash back to Cromwell Street. Of course, I never let him take me as far as the gate. I left him at the edge of the park and went the rest of the way on my own. This went on for some weeks until eventually I decided to risk approaching my parents about it. Phil was making me feel good; I was fifteen and I wanted to experience the fun other teenage girls were enjoying. I decided that my father was the one to ask and took a chance. At this time he was still regularly abusing me, but often he would reward me in some way afterwards. Sometimes the reward would take the form of just a little more freedom.

'Dad, would it be all right if I got home a little later after school? If I was home, say, half an hour afterwards instead of fifteen minutes? Then I could walk home with some of my friends.'

He gave me a shrewd look. 'I've told you before, Anna-Marie, it's dangerous out there. I don't want you walking the streets.'

'But I wouldn't be on my own, Dad. What if someone walked me all the way here?'

'Oh, so there's some fella sniffing round, is there? Some boy who wants to walk you home?'

I blushed, but I was determined to press on now that I had broached the subject. 'It's just a friend, Dad. Just a boy in my year. It's only an extra fifteen minutes. Can I?'

'All right, but only fifteen minutes. That should give you enough time to have it away in the park.' He laughed as if he had said something really funny.

I mumbled: 'He's just a friend.' But I knew when I had scored a small victory, and thought it wise not to press the point further.

Having given his permission for Phil to walk me home, my father wanted to have a good look at him. I can still remember the first day I brought him in for tea. I know Phil thought my family were a strange bunch from the very beginning. It was embarrassing for me but I couldn't go on making excuses not to introduce him, so one day, after checking with Fred and Rose that it would be OK, I invited him in.

Phil sat down at one end of the kitchen table and Dad and Rose at the other while I started making a cup of tea for everyone. They all just stared at each other and Phil looked a bit uncomfortable. After a while Fred leaned towards him and proffered a pack of cigarettes. 'Want a fucking fag?' he asked.

Phil's eyes widened but he kept a polite expression as he declined. It wasn't that he didn't smoke — most of the kids in school did. He was just amazed to be offered a cigarette by an adult and taken aback by the language. Even now you rarely hear Phil swear, and in those days he certainly didn't. That afternoon around the kitchen table Fred and Rose kept it up non-stop. It was f—ing this and f—ing that all the time. Despite my upbringing, or perhaps because of it, I have always tried to limit my use of that kind of language, too, and I was so ashamed. But Phil just kept plugging away, being so polite and so grown up and mature for a fifteen-year-old schoolboy.

After he left I looked at my father expectantly. I knew he would give an opinion without my asking and I didn't imagine it would be favourable. It wasn't.

'Well, he's a fucking divvy. You don't want no fucking schoolboy. Get a real man. You want someone who'll sort you out. He won't know what to fucking do with it.'

Rose laughed. 'Don't worry, I'll keep her busy. She won't have time for schoolboys.'

They looked at each other and grinned. 'Fucking divvy, that one,' Fred said again.

After that I got to see Phil quite regularly. I was allowed to walk home from school with him and to see him on Sundays. It was a much-appreciated support for me but it can't have been much fun for Phil. Sunday was major laundry day at our house in Cromwell Street and I was the one who had to do it all. Consequently our regular Sunday date was spent in the washroom, with me up to my eyes in it and Phil perched on a ledge chatting to me. I had to do all the other children's washing as well as Fred's and Rose's, and there were four sets of school uniforms to get ready for the following week.

It took an age, especially since we didn't have an automatic washing machine. I would get all hot and flustered and glow from the effort, but Phil never seemed to mind. He was just happy to be able to see me and sit and chat about school, life in general and his future plans which, I was glad to hear, seemed to always include me. It was a pleasant time when I could indulge in my own little dream world of how life might be. But it was never more than that, a dream; reality would come crashing back the moment he left.

We had a couple of proper dates, going to the cinema and things like that, but they were very rare because I simply wasn't allowed to go out. In desperation I sought permission to go to Phil's house to study for my exams in the evenings. We wanted to do our homework together. We managed a couple of evenings, and I remember sitting on the sofa at his house watching *Top of the Pops* on a Thursday, his little sister, who was four years younger, insisting on joining us. But when we tried to make a regular thing of it as the end of term approached we met another barrier. Phil's stepmother disapproved, and that was the end of that. While neither family really approved of the friendship, obviously they had very different reasons. Despite their own views, Fred and Rose didn't actually stop me having anything to do with Phil and he came in handy later when they needed someone to blame for that ectopic pregnancy. They just told the hospital authorities that I had been messing around with some boy at school. They didn't name names; instead Dad staged an act at my bedside, saying he wanted to see the young man I had been hanging round with and I had better make sure he knew it.

Out of the Shadows

To me the whole thing was confusing because of course I didn't know what was supposed to be wrong with me. But one day when Phil came to visit me and I was feeling really down I took it out on him. It was the first of many occasions when I tried to push him away, although deep down I knew I would hate it if he went. I felt I wasn't good enough for him and it would be better for both of us if he simply walked away. But Phil has never been one to give in easily. I told him: 'My dad wants to see you. He says you're to blame for my being here. He's going to have a right go at you.'

I didn't say it to him very nicely but Phil simply shrugged his shoulders and replied, 'OK, I'll go and see him.'

He did, too. When he left the hospital he marched straight round to Cromwell Street, feeling very brave and hard done by, and rang the doorbell. Luckily he was greeted by a rather sheepish-looking Rose, who told him Fred was out. Phil said to her bullishly: 'Well, I understand he wants to see me. What's the problem?' Rose feigned ignorance but Phil insisted, 'Tell him I want to see him, too, and I'll be back.' Phil told me many years later that afterwards he was as scared as hell at what he had done. But he felt so protective towards me and so upset that I had been nasty to him that he hadn't even stopped to think about how much older, bigger and stronger Fred was. He considered it later, though, and never carried out his threat to return. Not surprisingly, the matter was conveniently forgotten by Fred and Rose.

Phil was the best thing that had ever happened to me. My relationship with him made me feel almost normal although of course I knew I wasn't, or at least my life wasn't. But in spite of my deep feelings for him, even at that young age, eventually I pulled away from him. I had too much to deal with and too much I couldn't tell him. I was terribly ashamed of the way

I was forced to live at Cromwell Street and the things I was made to do, and of the abuse I suffered at the hands of my father. But I had never confided in anybody, and I couldn't begin with Phil. I was frightened of what he would make of it all. He might not believe it; he might blame me in some way. We were both so young and what was happening to me would be way outside his experience. So instead of turning to him I began to reject him. In some ways it was a form of self-destruction, but as I said, I felt I did not deserve him and that he would be better off without me. I had no self-worth, so how could I expect other people to value me?

In April 1980, just as our exams were approaching, we split up. It was my decision, not Phil's, and he was gutted. He felt as if he had been kicked in the teeth, and although I hated hurting him I was convinced I was doing the right thing. I could not let my heart rule my head and did what I believed I had to do. I made all sorts of excuses about why our relationship should finish: we were soon to leave school and would go our separate ways, anyway; his family didn't want to know me; my family didn't like him; we were too young — anything but the truth, whatever that was.

Of course, I missed him. I missed his uncomplicated company, the fact that he never made any demands on me, the laughs we shared, the dreams. That summer, after we had left school, I wrote Phil a letter and he got back in touch straight away. He came to visit me at Midland Road, where I was helping my dad with some building work. It wasn't easy to talk, but it was obvious that Phil was pleased to see me and I felt the same. Later that same summer I got a little job in a nearby bed-and-breakfast place and he came there to see me too. I had to go in early and cook the breakfasts for the guests, I waited on tables and cleaned and changed the beds later. It got me out of the house, for which I was grateful. But still my freedom was curtailed. My parents knew the hours I worked and expected me to be home at all other times. Phil came to see me at work on a couple of occasions and I risked being late home so that I could talk to him when I had finished. But the bed-and-breakfast place was only around the corner from Cromwell Street, so I was also in danger of being spotted with Phil.

It was wonderful seeing him again and we had lost none of our closeness, but just as before I began to feel it could never be. This time I didn't only push him away – I simply vanished altogether. I gathered my courage and ran away from Cromwell Street, from my father, from Rose, from the men who abused me and even from Phil. It would be nearly five years before our paths crossed again.

13

On the Run

The house was silent. I sat on the edge of my bed and took a few deep breaths. My heart was banging against my ribcage so loudly I thought it would wake everyone. I closed my eyes for an instant and summoned up the courage to carry out my plan. I had been waiting for a night like this for weeks. Fred and Rose had gone to bed quite early. There had been no visitors that evening and instead of going drinking they had stayed in and watched television. The younger children had long been asleep and I was the only one whose eyes had never closed. I didn't dare fall asleep in case I did not wake up in time to make my escape.

I had lain in bed for more than three hours turning everything over in my mind non-stop. It had to be tonight. Tonight the coast was clear and I could get away; I could start my new life the moment the door of 25 Cromwell Street closed behind me. I had to do it. I had to keep my nerve, and once I was through that door there would be no going back.

I considered the idea of freedom. I hadn't a clue what I would do with it, but already I could taste it. My mouth was dry. I moistened my lips nervously, stood up and out of habit straightened the covers on my wooden single bed. My clothes were draped over a wicker chair in the corner and I pulled them on. I had already stuffed a few things into a carrier bag and hidden it behind the chair. As I went to grab the bag I banged against the chair in my haste. I gasped, closed my eyes for a moment and listened for a sound which might mean I had been heard. Nothing. I glanced round the sparsely furnished room one last time. I wasn't leaving much behind: clothes I hated, a few ornaments, magazines, posters, the paraphernalia of a teenage girl.

I opened the door slowly, making no sound but a quiet brushing against the threadbare carpet. I headed for the stairs, missing out the floorboard on the landing which always creaked, and made my way to the front door. I slipped my feet into my shoes, which I had left there earlier, and slid the bolt. It made a slight grating sound but not enough to echo through the hall. I slipped the latch and, taking a deep breath, walked out into the night. Just one more obstacle to go. I shut the front door with a click and then tackled the big black iron gates which led to the street and liberty.

It was nearly three o'clock in the morning. The street lights gave off a dim glow and the sky was clear, promising another warm summer's day. I ran soundlessly along Cromwell Street, heading for the park. I wanted to whoop with joy. I had made it! I wanted to cry with terror, too, because I had no idea what to do next.

I had meticulously planned my escape but I had given little thought to anything else. I had nowhere to go, very little money and there was every chance that they would come looking for me. I sat on a park bench with my carrier bag of clothes and fought back the tears. I told myself that I was free; I would never go back, no one could abuse me again. No matter what happened from now on, it couldn't be any worse than my life so far. I sat there for hours and eventually I must have fallen asleep, because when I opened my eyes it was morning. The birds were singing and the sky was pink from the rising sun. I felt stiff, cold and damp with the dew, but now that the darkness had gone I wasn't quite so frightened. I knew I would survive somehow.

I headed for the public toilets in the park and had a wash. I straightened my clothes, combed my rather wild bushy brown hair and set off into town. I avoided the part of Gloucester frequented by Fred and Rose and found a café. A cup of tea and a slice of toast made me feel better, but I still hadn't formed any plans. All I knew was an intense sense of relief.

I understand now that if I had not run away when I did I would have left Cromwell Street the same way as my sister Heather — in a box covered by a black cloth carried by a grave-looking policeman in front of the world's press. I didn't know it then, or even suspect it, but there were at least seven, possibly eight, bodies buried around the house by the time I fled.

I learned later, from Heather, in fact, what happened on the morning after I ran away from home. When I didn't come down to prepare breakfast, Rose sent one of the younger children to look for me.

'She's not in her room or the bathroom. I can't find her.'

'Go and call her, Fred. She's your bloody daughter,' Rose snapped.

A few minutes later my father came back into the kitchen. His expression was set. 'Her bed's made but she's not there.

She's not in the house anywhere. I think she's done a runner.'

They exchanged angry looks. Rose said: 'Cow.'

'I don't think she'll be a problem, do you?' asked Fred.

Rose didn't answer, but the atmosphere was tense throughout breakfast.

Later that day my father and Rose went into my bedroom and stripped it bare. They tore my Elvis Presley posters off the walls, bundled up my magazines and books of pop lyrics and burned the lot. The rest of my clothes went too, even the ornaments on my shelves were thrown out. It was as if I had never exsisted.

I never regretted leaving but I felt guilty about leaving my younger brothers and sisters behind. I felt I had let them down, but I had no choice. I hadn't told any of them I was going to run away: I couldn't run the risk of one of them accidentally letting it out. I was terrified that Rose would find out what I was planning. I knew I would get the hiding of my life. Now I believe that they would simply have killed me, like they did Heather years later. Sometimes I would sneak along to the school and find my brothers and sisters and check that they were all right. I swore them to secrecy, but to make sure I was not caught I left a long time between visits in case Rose or Dad decided to wait around the school to try to find me.

Life on the streets was hard but it was still better than what I had known. No matter how bad things got I never felt the desire to go back home. I had been building up to fleeing for some time. After I left school, life at Cromwell Street had grown even more unbearable. I had the usual schoolgirl dreams of becoming an air hostess, seeing the world, or maybe working in a holiday camp. But I knew none of it would be possible if I stayed. Rose had already informed me that she expected me to stay at home and look after the younger children while she carried on her own 'business'. I loved them all but I felt it was unfair: I wanted a life of my own. Rose's idea was that I should have children. She loved babies and saw me as a kind of potential breeding machine. In my mind's eye my life stretched before me as one long round of babies and skivvying and abuse. There had to be another way.

I had made up my mind to leave soon after I got out of hospital after the ectopic pregnancy. One horrific incident strengthened my conviction. I had only been out of hospital a few days and still had clips and stitches holding the wound together. I remember walking around bent double and feeling crippled, but Rose insisted I did some light housework. I hardly felt up to it but I knew better than to refuse. As I dusted and polished and hoovered I kept glancing in her direction. I tried not to meet her eye but I recognised the signs. Something had upset her, nothing I did would be right. She was going to throw one of her fits. My heart sank, but I kept on cleaning.

Then she was behind me. 'You're not doing that right.' She shoved me as she said it.

I kept my head down. 'Sorry.'

'Don't be fucking sorry. Just do it fucking right.'

I said nothing and kept my face averted, but it wasn't good enough. She grabbed my shoulder and shook me, then pushed me to the floor. Pain erupted as I crashed against the furniture. Her face was a picture of evil, her eyes filled with rage but with that strange dead look behind them. 'Stupid cow. I'll teach you.' She began to kick me repeatedly in the stomach and I screamed as the pain ripped through me. I put my hands over my belly and tucked my head in to protect myself. Another well-aimed kick and she walked off. I struggled to my feet and headed for the stairs and my room. She screamed after me: 'You wait till your fucking father gets home.'

I locked the door and stayed there until he did, at 4 p.m. I could hear Rose briefing him on what had happened but I couldn't make out what she was saying. It didn't matter. Whatever story she told him was going to be miles from the truth, and he wasn't going to care much either way in any case. I just didn't want another beating from either of them.

I heard his footsteps coming up the stairs. They paused outside my room and then he banged on the door and tried the handle. 'Open the door, Anna-Marie. Open the bloody door.'

I resisted for a few moments while he knocked harder, and then I quietly opened it, my eyes downcast, my expression sullen. He came into the room. 'You shouldn't provoke and upset your mum like that.'

'I didn't. I didn't do anything.'

'Well, come downstairs, then, and have your tea.'

I shook my head. 'I'm staying here.'

He gave a sigh of exasperation. 'Anna-Marie, don't push it. Don't be stupid.'

I was overwhelmed by a feeling of powerlessness but managed a mutinous look.

'You're coming downstairs or I'll give you a bloody good hiding, too.'

I gave in and led the way downstairs to the kitchen, where I made everyone a cup of tea. The atmosphere was tense and awkward for the rest of the evening but I got through it.

Out of the Shadows

That night, when I went to bed, I sobbed quietly into my pillow and vowed I would get away.

I was sixteen years old, on the streets and on the run. That's how it felt. Every time I turned a corner or felt someone's eyes on me I was sure it would be Dad or Rose. My fear of that woman was so great that I was constantly looking over my shoulder. I don't know what I thought would happen if she found me. Perhaps I would be snatched off the street, taken back to Cromwell Street, and forced back into the life I hated. I didn't doubt they were capable of doing just that. My only chance was to keep out of their way.

I suppose I should have formulated more of a plan before I left, but the actual escape was all I could think about. After a few nights in the park I realised that had been a big mistake. I turned to a schoolfriend for help. Karen had been having problems and had managed to find herself a bedsit in Oxford Road. The place was tiny but it was warm and safe, and I was just glad of somewhere to rest my head. Unfortunately, her landlord didn't approve. The room was only meant for one and I was not paying rent. I had no job and was too frightened to try to sign on in case it led to Rose and Fred tracking me down. Karen would try to sneak me in when her landlord wasn't about, but one night there was an altercation which ended with him pushing me down the stairs. To stay any longer might have meant Karen losing her home so once again I was back on the streets.

I am greatly ashamed of this period of my life but I have begun to come to terms with why it turned out the way it did. You have to remember how I had been brought up and what I considered to be normal. My brain might have started to register the fact that other people didn't live the way we did at 25 Cromwell Street, but nonetheless it was still all I knew, the only kind of behaviour I had ever experienced. I associated everything with sex. The only kind of love and affection I ever knew came from my father after he had had sex with me. To get love, you had to provide sex; if someone gave you something or offered to help you in any way, you repaid them with sex. If you wanted something from someone, you offered them sex. To avoid beatings and provoking Rose, and to please her, you had sex with her or with the men she had chosen. That was the way my mind worked. I had been brainwashed by my father and Rose and by my own experiences into believing that this was the way of the world. So there I was, aged sixteen, naïve beyond belief but sexually way ahead of my years, with a desperate need of a roof over my head. To get it I used the only method I had — sex.

This was the early eighties and CB radios were at the height of their popularity. Everybody seemed to have one and there were hundreds of people in Gloucester calling up strangers for innocent and not-so-innocent daytime and late-night conversations. Karen had managed to get hold of a set and we spent hours chatting up blokes over the airways. It started as fun, but it became a way of finding places for me to stay.

I'm not going to name names, because a lot of the families I stayed with probably still live in Gloucester and there has been enough hurt and tragedy in that town because of Fred and Rose without my adding to it. Some of the people who put me up were very kind. The women of the house took me in because they felt sorry for me. Some had daughters my age. They helped me because they didn't like to think of their own daughters homeless and on the streets without someone doing the same for them. But it was the men who took advantage.

I would ask over the airwaves if there was anyone who could put me up for the night or for a few days. I was after any accommodation I could get. Anyone listening could tell I wasn't too fussy. Sometimes I spoke to girls my own age and they would ask their parents if their new friend could come and stay. Each time I would want it to be wonderful, the chance to become part of a real family, but it never happened. Of course I still had no money, and would be left alone in the house for much of the day. There were several family men who, in those circumstances, let it be known what they expected from a homeless young girl in exchange for their hospitality. They always got what they wanted.

I feel ashamed and humiliated about that now, but I knew no different then. It was expected of me and I always did what other people wanted. It was how I stayed alive. To some the way I lived must seem like prostitution. But I was never after money; I simply needed shelter and food.

After a few months I landed on my feet. I met a man (I'll call him Alan, though it's not his real name) over the airwaves who offered me a room in his home as a lodger. He was separated from his wife and wanted someone to do his housework in exchange for the room. It meant I had a proper address and could get social security and just enough money to live on. The house was not far from St Paul's School and I was able to intercept my younger brothers and sisters on their way there and back to check how they were. To be on the safe side I never told them where I was living. I was still wary of staying in Gloucester because Dad knew so many people there, but I didn't have enough cash or courage to move on.

I lived for some months with Alan and the arrangement worked well, but then his wife decided that they should have another try at making their marriage work and she moved back in. I had made friends with Alan's elderly mum, who lived nearby. She was in her late sixties or early seventies and treated me like a daughter. I used to help her with her cooking and cleaning and was genuinely fond of her — she was a lovely lady. When she learned that I was about to be homeless again she suggested that I lodged with her and carried on helping around the house. I was thrilled. At last somebody liked me for myself. I moved in and did everything I could for her. I was so happy. No one was abusing me; I had a roof over my head, enough money for food, and someone genuinely cared and expected little in return.

It was too good to last — and it didn't. Alan's wife used to visit her mother-in-law on a regular basis and was not amused to find me in residence. I knew she didn't like me being there and tactfully kept out of the way. Whenever she came round I would excuse myself and go to my room until she left, but it wasn't enough. There were arguments and tension and rather than cause trouble in the family, I left. I was back to square one: more men, more abuse, more tears, more moments when life didn't seem worth living.

I found a man I'll call Pete over the CB at a time when I was going from pillar to post. I met him for a drink. He was a lot older than me, but that didn't matter — most of the men who abused me were in their thirties and forties, and I was used to it. By now I was seventeen and little in my life had changed. Pete had a flat and he suggested I came and lived with him. Nothing was said at first, but I knew the deal. I got somewhere to live, food and warmth and he got sex. I moved in. It was OK for a while. I was an expert at switching off. Nothing much can hurt you when you are mentally numb most of the time.

But Pete wanted more than just sex: he wanted someone he could abuse when things weren't going right for him. He needed a whipping-boy. I took it for a while. Again it was nothing new: a few too many pints and I got a black eye; a badly judged word or phrase and I got two. But one night he beat me up badly. It was time to move on once again.

That night I got on the CB radio and spoke to a guy called Chris Davis. He was living in Stroud, a few miles from Gloucester. He was five years older than me and living with a woman in her thirties who had five children by someone else. A lodger who could help out with the kids seemed a good bet. I told Chris over the CB how much I wanted to leave the man I was with and why. He came over and even helped me move my stuff out. I moved in with Chris and his girlfriend — I'll call her Yvonne — as their lodger and that was how it stayed — until Chris started paying me too much attention. It was a bit of a strange set-up. I couldn't understand what a young guy like him was doing with someone so much older and with a ready-made family. I didn't want to rock the boat and I tried not to encourage him, but I was nearer his age and we got on quite well. It eventually became obvious to his girlfriend that his interest was more than just friendly. She said I had to go. 'Anne Marie, I want you out. I'm fed up with this. I know what's going on. I want you out. Now. Today.'

I didn't blame her and I wasn't going to make a fuss. 'OK. I'm sorry. I'll go.'

We were in the kitchen of the house in Stroud. It was a mess. I wouldn't miss it. But what happened next stunned me. Chris was making a cup of coffee. Without turning round, he said: 'She stays.'

'She bloody doesn't.'

Still with his back to both of us, he said quietly: 'If she goes. I go.'

I didn't want this. I told them, 'It's all right. It doesn't matter. I'll leave.' I went upstairs to my room and began packing my things into carrier bags. There still wasn't much: some clothes, make-up, cheap jewellery, toilet things, a few ornaments. The discussion below was getting noisy and I didn't want to be involved. I went downstairs and out of the front door, leaving my key on a table in the hall.

Chris was loading some things into his car, which was parked in the road. He had a small suitcase and some other bags of clothes. 'I've had enough. I'm going too. Can I give you a lift somewhere?'

I shook my head and headed off down the street. I heard the car door shut and the engine start. Moments later he pulled up a few yards ahead and got out of the car. 'Come on, chuck your stuff in the back and I'll drop you off somewhere.'

It seemed crazy not to, so I did as I was told and got into the passenger seat. We drove for a while in the direction of town, neither of us saying a word. Then he cast a quick look in my direction, pursed his lips and asked: 'So, are you going to stay with me, or what?'

For a while I said nothing. Various thoughts flashed fleetingly through my brain but it wasn't a tough decision. I had nowhere else to go.

'Yes. All right.'

We found lodgings that day at a pub in Gloucester which rented out rooms to people on social security. Chris wasn't working either, but we had a guaranteed income so the landlord was quite happy. I was sick of moving from pillar to post on my own. I stayed with Chris for the company –

Out of the Shadows

I wanted to feel I belonged somewhere. He took me to meet his mum. I felt he wanted me, so I stayed with him. I was too tired not to. And all of a sudden I wasn't on my own any more.

14

Marriage

We found lodgings at the Prince of Wales in Station Road, Gloucester for some months. It was being run partly as a guest house and the rent was paid for us by the DHSS. You weren't supposed to stay in your room all day so, as neither of us was working, we spent a lot of time just going up town and walking around. To earn a little bit of extra cash we occasionally helped out by serving in the bar or changing beer barrels in the cellar. Sometimes I helped the housekeeper clean the rooms and change the beds. It wasn't a very fulfilling existence but at least I had a roof over my head. I was still only seventeen and it was better than most of the situations I had known.

While we were at the Prince of Wales Chris regularly quizzed me about my family. I made non-committal replies to his questions, merely intimating that there had been something of a family row and we were no longer really in touch. I hadn't seen Dad or Rose since the day I ran away from Cromwell Street but I hadn't cut myself off completely. I still sent birthday cards to the children and even Mother's and Father's Day cards to Fred and Rose. Chris kept up the pressure. He wanted to meet my family and felt I should make it up with them. I had met his mother, after all, and he thought he should become acquainted with the Wests. I couldn't bring myself to fill him in on my background and the years of abuse I had suffered, although I tried to tell him that my parents had rather odd ways. It didn't put him off and so, feeling very nervous about it, I made a phone call to my father. There was no way I was simply going to turn up at Cromwell Street unannounced — the thought of even crossing the threshold left me cold with dread so I tested the water first.

My dad seemed pleased to hear from me, although we only had a short conversation the first time I called.

'Dad. It's Anna-Marie, Dad.'

'Anna. Bloody hell. You all right, girl?'

'I'm fine, Dad. I was just ringing to say hello and to tell you I'm OK. How are the children?'

'They're all fine. Why are you ringing now. What's up?'

'Nothing. I told you, I just thought I would get in touch.'

'Left it long enough, didn't you. Where are you, then?'

There was a bit more of the same. I told him I would ring again and hung up. The next time I called I told him I had a steady boyfriend and that we were living together in Gloucester, but I didn't say where. There were a few more phone conversations before I told my father Chris wanted to meet the family. Straight away Dad invited us round, though he had to consult Rose about the arrangement first and it took another call before we fixed a date and time. Nevertheless I felt quite strongly that I didn't want to go, but Chris insisted. I was very tense on the way there and so nervous. I thought the atmosphere when we arrived was full of tension, too, but it might just have been me. My father was very welcoming, but that was often his way when anybody new came to the house. He would be all friendly while he worked out whether they would be of any use to him.

Rose was just Rose. She was always the same. She never put on any airs or graces when people visited. If she was in a bad mood when you got there she stayed in a bad mood, and you could take it or leave it. But that day she was polite and reasonably friendly, although she didn't say much.

We went straight into the kitchen when we arrived and Rose put the kettle on.

'Dad, this is Chris.'

'All right, mate?' My father shook his hand roughly.

My mouth was dry with nerves but I managed to carry on the introductions. 'Chris, this is my dad, Fred, and my stepmum, Rose.' I got a bit of a look for that but I had already decided that I could not introduce her as my real mother.

Rose stayed near the sink, busying herself, while Dad, Chris, and I sat at the kitchen table drinking mugs of tea. There were no questions about where I had been for the previous two years or so or why I had left, and I didn't offer any explanations. There were some strained silences as we all tried to think of something to say, but we managed. In the end Dad began to quiz Chris about himself.

'What do you do then, son?'

'Well, I'm not working just now. But I do a bit of this and that.'

I could see that my father was not impressed. He liked

to meet people with a trade so that he could persuade them to do something around the house or ask them to get him something at trade price. If Dad met a carpenter he would soon have some free wood, a bricklayer and he came home with bricks.

'Well, do you want a bit of work? I could find you something you could help me with for a few quid.'

They talked about it for a while and that was that. The visit lasted barely twenty minutes but I was ready to be off. I had been terrified of going back but I felt safe because Chris was with me. I didn't want to be drawn back into the fold but I found I still wanted to keep in touch with my dad. I saw him several times after our visit to the house, mainly meeting him in town, and steadily I was brought back under the influence of Cromwell Street once again. Dad found Chris odd jobs here and there and when he discovered we were living in bed-and-breakfast accommodation he sorted us out a bedsit with facilities just down the road at number 31.

Chris and I began to fight even before we moved into our new home near my family. Drink was usually involved and living in a pub didn't help. We had a lot of arguments over money, mainly because we didn't have any. Chris wanted to spend what little we had on drink and cigarettes. I would argue that there were other things we could do with.

One night, after a particularly heavy drinking session and a terrible argument, we clashed so furiously that I went crashing across the small bedroom head-first into the wardrobe. The impact of hitting such a solid piece of furniture left me totally deaf. I had no hearing at all for several weeks. Fortunately, it suddenly came back.

Many women would have walked out on such a marriage,

but you have to understand I never expected a normal relationship. And in any case, I had no one to turn to and nowhere else to go. So we moved into Cromwell Street and tried to make ends meet the best we could. Helping my father with his building work as a child paid dividends, and every now and then I got some work as a builder's labourer through a family friend. Chris said he had arthritic knees, which meant some jobs were difficult. They did not however prevent him from riding the huge motorbike his mother had lent him the money to buy.

I was thrilled when I discovered that I was pregnant with Michelle. I had always loved children and I wanted to have them myself. I didn't really consider Chris much in the equation; I was just pleased that I was going to have a baby of my own. It came as something of a shock when I realised that everyone expected us to get married – and before the baby was born. Chris's mum in particular was keen we should do the right thing. She said it was only proper and Chris didn't object.

I didn't want to get married. I had always said I never would, and I felt that in this day and age there was no reason to. But I was overruled by both families and as usual I did as I was told. It just seemed to happen: your hormones are all over the place when you are pregnant and I found myself going with the flow. Even though I knew in my heart that it would never work out and it was the wrong thing to do, one day I just found myself getting married.

It was 14 January 1984 and the ceremony took place at Gloucester Register Office. I can't help laughing when I think of that day. It was the most ridiculous wedding ever and I was hardly the traditional bride. There were no posh cars or a long flowing dress and veil, and no bridesmaids. Chris's family were all there, but only my father and another relative turned up to represent the Wests. Rose said that all my younger brothers and sisters had come down with the mumps and she had to stay at home to look after them. I don't think it was true: one or two of them certainly weren't well, but I think she just used it as an excuse not to come.

I was very nervous and I wasn't sure quite what to expect. I wore a silver-grey, white and black striped maternity dress with a white padded quilt coat and a carnation from my bouquet in my hair. I did my own hair and make-up and made up the bouquet myself. They weren't real flowers, they were fake, made of some sort of material, but at least they weren't plastic. The petals were pink and white and the whole thing was finished off with a pink ribbon and bow. I remember I liked them very much. The neighbours must have had a good old giggle as my father and I set off for the wedding. There I was, pregnant in my new dress, and there was Dad looking all uncomfortable in his three-piece grey suit, which was too big and had flared trousers, and sporting a wide patterned tie.

We were arguing as we walked along Cromwell Street and I could see people we knew watching us. We were both a bit embarrassed and neither of us wanted to carry the bouquet. I kept saying, 'No, you carry it. Hide it under your jacket.' Dad kept pushing it back at me and we were arguing and laughing at the same time. When we arrived at the register office Chris and his family were amazed to find we had walked there. They kept saying we should have asked them for a lift and we assured them that it wasn't far to walk. Chris didn't look much like a groom, either. He had insisted on wearing his black satin bomber jacket, but at least he was wearing a tie with it!

Out of the Shadows

Even the ceremony was a bit of a farce. Chris got an old pal of his to act as best man. He got the ring stuck on his finger and everyone laughed. Afterwards we all stood around outside. We hadn't booked an official photographer and the family had to take their own pictures. There's one of me with my arm through Dad's. I'm smiling at the camera and he has a fixed grin on his face and is all stiff and uncomfortable. There are other photographs taken during the actual wedding service. We all look very serious. The rest of the snaps were taken at the reception. It was held, at my father's insistence, in the basement at Cromwell Street. I shudder when I look at those pictures now. To think that there we all were, drinking sherry and eating wedding cake over the bodies of five women murdered by Fred and Rose.

Of course, we knew nothing about any of that that day. We simply arrived back at the house and handed out glasses of sweet sherry to our guests. My mother-in-law had asked a friend of hers to make the cake. It had two tiers and we had to use three knives to get through the icing. It was very thin but had set hard, and our attempts to cut it caused much amusement. There were no speeches and only a few presents. Dad and Rose gave us some tea towels and two Pyrex dishes. The reception only lasted about an hour and then we simply walked off down the street back to our bedsit and carried on as normal.

It was a pauper's wedding and it meant little. We only did it for the sake of convention and to keep other people happy. All I wanted was someone to make me feel secure, somebody who could put a protective film around me, but instead I merely succeeded in immersing myself in another nightmare and surrendering control of my life again. I didn't ease any burdens. I know now that getting married was the wrong thing to do and I am sorry if saying so upsets people. But I have told Chris many times I should never have married him, and if he is honest he probably agrees. The one good thing that came out of it all is our daughter Michelle, and I shall never regret having her.

Michelle was born on 17 June 1984, which was Father's Day that year. Chris and I were invited to my family's house for Sunday dinner. We all sat around the table for a traditional Sunday roast cooked by Rose with the help of the younger children. After we had eaten I sat on the settee in the living room feeling quite tired. I lay back with my head in Chris's lap feeling very strange. The house was really quiet. My father was lying on the floor, sound asleep. He could sleep anywhere, my dad — he just dozed straight off. Rose was in the kitchen clearing up with my brothers and sisters. I began to feel restless and unwell. Rose appeared at the door just as I sat up. 'Are you all right? You don't look right.'

'No. I feel—'

I didn't know what I felt, but at that moment, as I stood up, my waters broke all over the sofa.

For once in her life Rose was kind to me. She took me into the bathroom and helped me change. She had had so many children herself that she knew exactly what to do. Chris went back to our bedsit and picked up the bag which was all packed and ready and the two of us walked to the hospital. Four hours later Michelle was born. She weighed 7lbs 12oz and was beautiful. My father and Rose came to visit. They brought flowers and a card. The card was lovely: it showed a picture of a baby which looked just like Michelle. It was so lovely I actually framed it and kept it.

When my husband and all my visitors had gone I lay back

Out of the Shadows

in my hospital bed and realised that I was a mother. It was hard to come to terms with. Never having really known my own mother, the only example I had was Rose, and I knew, no matter what, that I was going to be as far removed from her as was possible. My daughter would never suffer as I had.

I got out of bed and went to look at my little girl. She was in an incubator and I couldn't stop staring at her. I thought: 'That's mine, all mine. I can take her home and no one is going to take her away from me.' I felt an overwhelming feeling of love for that little bundle. She was depending on me. I was frightened but at the same time I was sure I wouldn't let her down, not ever. This was my family, mine; the very first thing that was all my own. I loved her unreservedly.

Unfortunately, I didn't love her father and our relationship did not improve after the baby was born. If anything it got worse. The arguments became stronger and I was torn between staying and leaving. I was still trying to discover some kind of hidden strength. If I had any at that time it was deeply buried.

Now when we fought there was Michelle to consider. On one occasion my tiny daughter became trapped in the middle of a furious row over Chris's drinking. I had decided I had had enough and was on the point of walking out. Chris refused to allow Michelle to go with me. There was a horrific tug of war: with him refusing to let her go and me trying desperately to snatch her from him.

'She's mine! She comes with me!' I screamed at him.

He held on. 'If you go, you go without her!' he yelled back.

'Give me my daughter.' I was frantic but he would not release her.

We battled and the abuse flew. Michelle screamed her head off and I became more and more desperate.

Finally I fled from the grotty bedsit, leaving Michelle behind, and dashed the few hundred yards up the road to get my father. Fred came back to the house with me and persuaded Chris to hand over the baby. I calmed her down and we all calmed down ourselves and of course I stayed. I don't know where I thought I was going to go when I threatened to pack my bags.

The cash we got from the social security and the occasional wages I brought in from labouring were not enough to keep us in food, clothes and cigarettes and Chris in drink. By this time Michelle was a few months old. I had no money to buy her a cot, nappies, clothes, food and all the things babies need. I developed a friendship with a man living locally. Chris knew about it, but said nothing. I'm not proud of it but this gentleman did help me out with things for my little daughter.

It wasn't that difficult: I had been doing it for years under Fred's and Rose's guidance, I had done the same thing on the road in order to survive, and now it was simply a case of having to do it again. Dad always said that women never had to go without; Rose told me no one ever gave you anything for nothing or liked you for what you were, only for what you could give them. I followed their philosophy. It is an episode in my life which I don't like to dwell on.

We waited our time on the council's housing list and eventually we were rewarded with a three-bedroomed semi on Gloucester's White City estate. It's not what you would describe as an upmarket area, but at least it was a proper home. It had a reasonable-sized kitchen, a downstairs bathroom and a large living room. It also had a big garden with plenty of room for Michelle to play. I was thrilled with the house and set about making it a real home. I did the painting and decorating myself. I'm no expert but I was proud of my efforts. I even put my building skills to work and constructed a stone surround and chimney breast for the fireplace. But no amount of home comforts were going to change the way Chris and I felt about each other.

One night, after yet another all-out screaming match, he lost his temper completely. One of his favourite possessions, a legacy of his martial arts phase, was a real Samurai sword. In blind fury he swung the lethal weapon at our bedroom door, the razor-edged sword sliced straight through it. The damage is still there to this day. I'm sure he didn't intend any real harm with it, he was just venting his temper.

Chris and I finally split up in 1990. By this time I had another daughter, Carol, who was three years old. Chris was not her father. I had met up once again with my childhood sweetheart, Phil, and the result was Carol. I had admitted as much to Chris, but we stayed together and at first he treated her as his own. I don't know if or when I would have found the courage to leave if Chris had not done so first. Later he tried to come back, but by then I had discovered that I could take charge of my own life.

I realised not long after our move that Chris was taking full advantage of his role as a house-husband. I would be out labouring and he would be at home complaining about his painful knees and holding coffee mornings. The guests were always female. I was amazed when in 1990 he found himself a job with a delivery firm. He talked a lot about one of his colleagues, an Asian girl who was having boyfriend problems.

One evening he announced that he was bringing her home

after work. This was unprecedented and I was surprised. I tidied the house, myself and the girls and welcomed her with the offer of a cup of tea. We were all very sociable and she even had her photograph taken with my daughters. Chris continued to refer to her as a friend with whom he worked. As my twenty-sixth birthday approached I discovered that this woman's birthday was just three days later. There was quite a difference in the way each of us marked our respective milestones. I spent my special day sitting on the sofa crying while Chris went to bed claiming stomach pains, not even acknowledging that there was anything to celebrate. He made a miraculous recovery for his new friend's birthday, and after taking a telephone call he announced that he would be out for the evening.

'Where are you going. Anywhere nice?' I tried to keep my voice casual, sensing I would find out more if I didn't make a fuss.

'Oh, I'm just taking her out for a drink.'

'Is she all right or is something wrong?'

'She's got boyfriend problems. I'm just going out for a chat and to console her a bit, you know.'

I shrugged and didn't comment further. The girl arrived at the house at about 6.30 p.m., came in for few minutes, and then they left. Chris arrived back home at 12.30 a.m.

I had spent the evening mentally debating my tactics. I didn't really care what he got up to but I wasn't going to be taken for a complete fool.

'How was your friend?' I asked.

'Oh, fine. OK.' He wasn't too forthcoming and avoided looking at me. Then he added: 'But she says next time she won't come in. I'll meet her outside and we'll go from there.'

I carried on pretending to put away the washing up in the kitchen. 'So she's sorted everything out with her boyfriend then, has she?'

'Yeah. She has.'

I gave him a slow considered look and, in a very level voice, remarked, 'You've got lipstick on your face.'

His hand immediately shot up to rub it off. 'Well, I gave her a bit of a kiss and a cuddle and held her hand. You know, just to console her.'

'That's nice. So how long has she been splitting up from her boyfriend?'

He didn't look at me as he moved out of the kitchen and headed towards the stairs. Over his shoulder he threw, 'Six months. About six months.'

I could feel the tears rising and the tension building. I snapped: 'Well, you made an effort for her but you couldn't make one for me for my birthday.'

He didn't reply, but as I got ready for bed I could see the anger in his eyes. I didn't want a fight; I felt too vulnerable so instead I opted for an attempt at reconciliation using the only method I knew. I had sex with him.

The next day I realised what a fool I was. I had thought everything would be calm and back to normal, but instead Chris said to me: 'Come on, I'm taking you down the bank.'

I was puzzled. He didn't have an account, but I did. 'Why. What do you want?'

'You're going to get me some money out.'

'What for? What do you want to buy?'

His answer stunned me. 'I'm going away for a few days. I need to think things through and decide what I want.'

I stood there open-mouthed, just gaping at him. 'What,

just like that? After last night? You're treating me like a whore.'

'Look, just get me the money. I'm going and I'll be back when I'm good and ready. I need a few days. Got it?'

So I did it. I went to the bank, gave him £100 and off he went. A few days later he telephoned. 'So are you coming back?' I demanded.

'No. I don't know. I don't know what I want to do.'

'Well, you either are or you're not. Which is it?'

'I don't know. I'm distressed. I'm confused. I don't know.'

This was not the first time he had taken off for a few days, usually after a row, and then he'd come home with nothing said. 'Chris, are you coming back?' I shouted.

'No.'

'Right. You don't come back at all, then.' I slammed down the phone.

I don't think he believed I meant it, and I was astonished myself to find that I did. I had the locks changed and that was it. I decided I was going to make my own way in life; I wasn't going to stay in a relationship which was wrong for me, not even for the sake of my children. In any case, I felt that they would be better off as well. I didn't want them to be brought up in an atmosphere of violence as I had been.

My decision was not popular with Chris's family, but I stuck to it — even when he came back and tried to persuade me otherwise. I stuck to my guns and Chris moved in with his mother. I don't know what happened to the relationship with his friend from work and I never bothered to ask. We managed to sort out who got what and he took all the electrical equipment from the house. I didn't argue, I just let him have it. Our settee had been given to us by his mother

Out of the Shadows

and I even gave that back. I got a friend with a trailer to take it to her house and we dumped it in the front garden. My father lent me one until Rose demanded it back to give to my half-sister Mae. After that the children and I sat on the floor for a while until I had saved up enough to buy a sofa of our own.

Everything in the house now is ours. We earned it in the proper way. We don't owe anything to anybody, and I never want to – I have respect for myself now. I suppose I learned it from Phil.

In losing Chris I found myself. I was a jumpy fat cow when he went. I had forgotten who I was, if I ever knew. I had lost my character, my personality, everything. My doctor tells me I was a hypochondriac when I was with Chris. It was my way of crying for help. I was at the doctor's surgery so often I might as well have had a season ticket. If it wasn't for me, it was for the children: I was a smother mother. If the slightest thing was wrong with them I panicked and rushed for medical help.

After Chris left I emptied my medicine cabinet. It took some time. Now all I have in it is TCP and Nurofen. I gave up smoking and went on a diet. I changed from a fat, unhappy woman into one in charge of her own life. At last I saw a light at the end of the tunnel. Even subsequent events and the revelations about my father and stepmother have not succeeded in extinguishing that completely. For the first time in my life I was responsible for myself, and, more importantly, for two other people. Now it was me and my two little girls against the world. It was terrifying, it was worrying, but it was exciting too. We didn't have much to keep us going, but it was enough. With two tots and no family support I wasn't able to just go out and get a good job and, let's face it, I wasn't exactly trained for anything, either. But at least we had a roof over our heads and I wasn't too proud to claim the benefits that helped to clothe and feed us.

It was intoxicating not to have to answer to anyone else. All my life I had been acquiescent and subservient to someone. First my father and Rose, then the men who abused me when I ran away from home, and then Chris. Now when I got up in the morning there was no one there to give me orders, to threaten me, to rule me. Bit by bit I found my feet. If sometimes it was a struggle, I loved the sensation of being my own woman. I'm not saying I turned into Superwoman overnight, but I did experience a kind of freedom I had never known and gradually I developed enough confidence to run with it. I still lavished love and attention on my girls to make up for the childhood I never had, but I was easier with them; I fussed less and allowed my own natural sense of humour and fun to come through. Fun? That was a new idea, too.

Little by little I got the house together again. I did it all myself. If a room needed decorating, I did it. If the wallpaper was a bit out of line, who cared? If I wanted something for the living room, kitchen or children's bedrooms I economised and saved up for it. We didn't live in a palace but we didn't live in a hovel, either, and most importantly, we were happy. It was as if I had been given a new start, the chance to live life like other normal people did. OK, so we were a one-parent family, three girls without a man about the house, but for me it was a break from the manipulative male-dominated existence of my previous life.

And for the first time I was meeting a man on my own terms. I was beginning to enjoy a grown-up relationship with someone who saw me as a partner, not a slave; as a friend, not a victim to be pushed around. Phil and I were gently edging back into each other's lives. We were both wary, but we had an understanding based on a past friendship which had never really faltered. I was enjoying my freedom but if there was anyone with whom I wanted to share a little of it, it was Phil.

15

Phil

Michelle was in her pushchair and Chris was with me when I met Phil again. We were shopping in Gloucester and all of a sudden there he was standing in front of us. I felt sick with shock. All the old feelings came rushing back and I was speechless for a few moments. I blushed with embarrassment and shame: I was overweight, I knew I looked rough, and I could see from Phil's expression what he thought of Chris. He looked at me with a kind but guarded expression, smiled a little sadly and said simply: 'Hello, Anne. It's been a long time.'

I didn't know how to respond. I just went red, stammered hello and said, 'This is Chris.' I didn't have to say any more. Phil immediately glanced down at my hand and saw the wedding ring. Instinctively I began to play with it, twisting it round my finger, almost trying to hide it. I didn't know where to look. I made an attempt at conversation but it all came out wrong. At the same time I was shocked to find that the intuition we had once shared was still there. I could tell what Phil was thinking and I knew he was reading my body language and thoughts, too.

Of course we've discussed this meeting many times since, which has only confirmed our impressions of what the other was thinking. Phil told me all he wanted to say was: 'God, Anne, what have you ended up with?'

I just wanted to tell him, 'I'm sorry. It's all been out of my control. This isn't the real me.'

Phil revealed later that he knew instantly there was no real affection between me and Chris, despite the evidence of Michelle. But even though he still had feelings for me he would have preferred to have found me with someone who loved me and whom I loved back; he felt I deserved someone who would love and care for me. I suppose the problem was I never thought I deserved it. What hurt Phil even more was knowing that he could have loved and cared for me himself — and that he wanted to.

He went away that day telling himself, 'That's it, then. It's over. That's the end of it. There's no point going on dreaming.' He thought about me a lot over the next week or so and then tried to put me out of his mind and his life forever. But, just like me, he left a little part of himself behind that day and deep down he knew that he would never forget, or want to.

The thought of our chance meeting never left me. I didn't like to think about it too often because it was a reminder of what might have been, and that was something I couldn't dwell on. Phil had been probably my one and only chance to live a life like other people and to experience a real and honest love. We both feel that our relationship were meant to be, but the path hasn't been easy.

Out of the Shadows

We did not meet again until the following year. It was fate, and it marked the beginning of a chain of events which resulted in the friendship and relationship we have now. I knew where Phil was working — don't ask me if it was a coincidence that I passed his shop as he was leaving work one evening or whether I subconciously sought him out, I don't know. It just happened.

It was beginning to get dark and it was raining. It was a miserable, cold night and I had my head lowered against the rain, battling to hold my coat together as the wind whipped it open. Phil was just driving out of the shop car park and we saw each other. We had the briefest of chats. I wouldn't get in the car: I made an excuse that I was on my way somewhere and that was it. But I had done it; I had seen him again, and I couldn't get him out of my mind. I thought about it all for a while and then, some days later, I picked up the telephone and called him at work. I kept it light; I told him I had been pleased to see him again. Would he mind if I rang occasionally for a chat, or perhaps we could have a drink for old times' sake?

We met in a local pub. I wouldn't let him pick me up; instead I walked there, unsure about what sort of reception I would get but excited at the chance to renew the one friendship in my life that had counted. No fireworks went off, no cymbals clashed — we just sat there like any other couple, had a few drinks, talked about the old days, laughed at some of things we had done as teenagers, and caught up on news of other old classmates. But it felt so good.

We began to see each other every couple of weeks. I would phone Phil at work and we would meet for a drink. It was no more than that. He thought it was strange that my husband didn't seem to mind if I went out with another man, and it was hard to explain that Chris cared very little about what I did. Eventually I gave Phil my phone number and address and if Chris answered when he rang he would be friendly and chatty, almost as if Phil were a pal of his, too. Phil would be thinking: 'I'm taking your wife out for a drink. Why aren't you upset about it?' I couldn't tell him then that Chris would encourage me to do anything if he thought there might eventually be some benefit in it, and besides, as neither of us was working and he couldn't afford to take me out, it at least got one of us out of the house.

For the first six months or so Phil and I kept things on an uncomplicated level. We were just old schoolfriends and that is how we treated each other. But we both knew it was more than that. Bubbling under the surface there was always something else. We avoided talking about our feelings; instead we had a drink, an occasional meal, played darts or pool at the pub, went to the cinema. The outings increased, becoming weekly, and they were the highlight of a dreary life for me.

Eventually we acknowledged our emotions. The feelings were so strong we couldn't hide them anyway, but we still didn't talk about it. We didn't have to: as I said, we have always known what the other was thinking. Phil was becoming more and more like part of the family. Now he came to the house and took Michelle out as well as me. We went on day trips to Alton Towers, for drives or picnics. For me it was a wonderful break from life with Chris. We had been living in each other's pockets twenty-four hours a day, and it had become obvious to both of us that we should never have married.

Things changed after Phil took Michelle and me on a week's holiday to a caravan site in Devon. Afterwards Chris

Out of the Shadows

pressured me to stop seeing Phil. Ruled by fear and the threat of violence, I initially did as I was told, but my feelings for Phil were so strong that even my fear was not enough to prevent me from contacting him. Within a matter of weeks we had taken up where we left off. But this time it was different. I threw caution to the winds. I desperately wanted another child, but I wanted it to be Phil's child. I worked out when the time was right and closed my mind to the consequences. For Phil it must have been a confusing period. He thought it would be the final straw for my marriage and set me free, but he was also wary because of all the times I had told him I didn't want him and sent him away. To me the reasons had been logical — it wouldn't work, I wasn't worthy of him — but to anyone else they spelled out 'unreliable' and 'confused'.

So Carol was conceived, and I was delighted. I was frightened, too, of course, but thrilled that I was carrying the child of the man I loved. Not surprisingly Chris was less impressed. For the first time ever in my life I had kicked against those who controlled me and rebelled, but such was my conditioning that eventually I gave in and toed the line once again. Life at home was awful. The violence unbearable but I felt I had no choice but to put up with it. Chris said he would accept the child as his and that I was to stay. He stood next to me while I telephoned Phil and told him of 'my' decision.

'I can't see you any more.'
'Why not?'
'I'm staying with Chris.'
'But the baby . . . there's only a few weeks to go.'
'Chris will accept the baby as his. I can't see you again. I don't want to see you again.'
'I don't believe you. Meet me. Say it to my face.'

'No, I can't see you.'

'You can't tell me to my face because you know I'll see you don't mean it.'

Chris ripped the phone from my hand. 'She doesn't want you. Now, fuck off.'

I gave birth to Carol on 24 February 1987 after a thirteen-minute labour. She weighed 6lbs 12oz. At one point they had been unable to find her heartbeat, but although she was a little sickly when she was born she survived. She suffers from asthma, eczema and hay fever now, but she copes well and the doctors keep an eye on her. About a month after she arrived I persuaded Chris to let me phone Phil. It was a tense and nervous conversation. He had made his own inquiries, and already knew that I had had a little girl, how much she weighed and when she was born. We were very tentative with each other but I invited him to come and see his daughter and told him her name.

It was a fraught visit. Chris was there so it didn't last long, and I cried when Phil had gone – I was so moved to see him with our daughter. I wanted to tell him that I hadn't meant any of the things I had said. It wasn't me talking, not the real me. I was just so frightened.

Over the next few years, before Chris left, Phil became a regular visitor to the house to see Carol. Our relationship was different; we behaved differently towards each other. We had to. Phil found it hard to trust me and I was still dominated by fear and unable to articulate what I felt. We became like brother and sister, and Phil assumed the role of a favourite uncle who came to see us and played with the children. He was always careful not to show any favouritism towards Carol and gave as much to Michelle as he did to his own daughter in terms of affection as well as material gifts.

At Christmas time Chris and I never had very much money, and it was Phil who bought the big presents for the girls. They were left under the tree as if they came from Father Christmas. Some time over the holiday season he would appear with a small gift for each of them from Uncle Phil. Between us we invented the Birthday Owl as the provider of the expensive presents they got on those special days, and once again Phil would appear with another small gift as befitted a family friend.

As luck would have it, from an early age Carol never saw eye to eye with Chris. They simply didn't get on. And Michelle, too, enjoyed Phil's company. He would pop in on his day off to play with both girls and chat to me. But he was so wary; the atmosphere between us was always strained and I knew I couldn't push it. I had hurt him badly on two occasions and if it happened a third time I knew I would lose him forever. He was so involved with Carol, and he was worried that relationship might be taken away from him at any minute.

The day Chris went for good I called Phil and told him. He didn't really believe it, and doubted it would be permanant. He was working away in Bristol at the time and dropped in when he could. When he realised that Chris really had gone he was very kind. He phoned or came round regularly to make sure that the girls and I were safe. Sometimes when I was worried or nervous he would sleep over on the sofa. He was there for me; we were friends.

The move back to our previous relationship was a gradual thing. Phil constantly wanted to know if I felt I had made the right decision in splitting up with Chris. He didn't want me to make another mistake; he wanted me to be sure of what I wanted and felt I needed time on my own to establish my own identity. He was right, but it was scary stuff. My relationship with Chris had deteriorated to the level experienced by many couples during a divorce, but he was allowed to see the children. He began to threaten to tell Carol about her parentage so Phil and I took the decision to tell her ourselves. We thought it would be better to break it to her gently in a way a five-year-old could understand. Michelle, too, would need to know.

So Phil sat them down on the sofa one day and told them a love story about a young couple who had been childhood sweethearts and had been all lovey-dovey like in the films. They had been separated but got back together again and had a little girl, and eventually they all came together as a family. The girls caught on quickly and Carol was delighted to discover that Phil was her father. She immediately started calling him Dad. For Michelle it was more difficult. She was bemused because Phil wasn't her father as well. At first she seemed to accept it all, but as she got older she resented the situation and sought out her own dad more. That was only natural, and we did all we could to make things work, but it hasn't been easy.

Since Carol learned about the situation she has expressed a great interest in being a bridesmaid, and of course it is her parents' wedding at which she longs to shine. We talk about the idea, but the last two years have not been an ideal time to consider it properly. The trauma over my father and stepmother have made our relationship stronger: we have closed ranks and become a small family unit and Phil has been my rock. But the next move is up to him. I have already proposed to him once – and he turned me down.

Out of the Shadows

It was Valentine's Day in a leap year and I planned the evening with great care. I wore my favourite outfit, sprayed myself with perfume and arranged for the children to sleep over with their friends across the road. I did everything I had ever read about in magazines to create a romantic atmosphere: I cooked a special meal, I laid the table beautifully and added a red rose in a glass vase; I bought champagne. It was only a half-bottle, and I could barely afford that, but it was the real thing. When Phil came round that evening he was greeted by the full works – soft music, subdued lighting, everything. I served his favourite meal and waited for the right moment – the moment when we could open the champagne and celebrate being together at last. I wasn't sure I would have the courage to go through with it. I had no second thoughts, but I was just so nervous.

He must have guessed what was coming, and in his own quiet way he let me ask him before telling me gently why he didn't think we should marry just yet. 'Anne, you're asking for a lot of commitment. It isn't just about now. It's about the future. As far as I'm concerned, marriage is a one-off thing. You have to be sure this is what you want.'

I had been terrified that he would say no but I was also sure that he loved me as much as I loved him, so I wasn't ready to be turned down. 'It is what I want.'

'You can't be sure. You don't know what you want. You don't know who you are. You need time and space to find out. You don't know what it's like to be free to make your own decisions. You deserve the chance to find out.'

I couldn't find the words to answer him and I could feel tears forming.

'Anne, I'm not saying I'll never marry you. But you have

to come to terms with who you are and we have to be sure it will hold together.'

I meant it when I told him: 'I'll never ask you again. If it's ever going to happen, it's up to you next time.'

He held me for a long time and I felt we at least had an understanding, if nothing else. But I still have that bottle of champagne, and maybe one day we'll open it.

16

Why?

I only once dared to ask my father: 'Why?' It was at a time when I felt really low and wanted to put my life into some perspective and order. I was twenty-three years old. I had just had a full hysterectomy following Carol's birth, which meant no more children. I was grateful for my two beautiful daughters, but it was still very distressing. I now knew that my gynaecological problems stemmed from the abuse I had suffered in my childhood and teens. I was old enough to understand how wrong and warped my life had been and I needed an explanation from the people responsible.

I sat in bed, propped up by a bank of pillows, and considered my past and my future. My bed had been brought down to the living room because I was so poorly I couldn't manage the stairs. I was still living with Chris, and he brought me the telephone so that I could call my father. I asked Dad and Rose to come and visit me but I didn't tell them why. It was quite a while since we had met so I just said

I had been in hospital, that I still wasn't well and wanted to see them.

They came late one afternoon. I had managed to get out of bed, dress in loose-fitting clothes and apply a little bit of make-up to help me face the ordeal. I sat on a comfortable chair in my living room, leaving the sofa for them. Chris made everyone a cup of tea because I wasn't even well enough to lift a full kettle.

'I've had a full hysterectomy, Dad. I can't have any more children.'

He avoided my eyes. 'You're all right, though. You're looking a bit peaky but you'll be OK. They wouldn't have let you of that hospital otherwise, would they?'

'I'm very sore and it's going to be a while before I can do much, even about the house,' I told him.

'And you've got two kids, haven't you? You don't need no more. They're lovely kids, them two.'

Rose was saying nothing, just looking down at the floor. Perhaps she guessed why I had invited them.

'Yes, but I could have had more if I hadn't been damaged when I was younger.'

My father ignored this. 'She's a lovely baby, your Carol. She looks like you did when your dad used to take you to work with him in your little cot.'

I wasn't going to be put off. I had courage now I had never possessed before. I was a mother twice over and had the protection of Chris being in the house, even if our relationship was nearly over.

'Dad, I have to know why. I want to know why you did all those things to me when I was young. Why did you do it, Dad? You must have known it was wrong. You don't do things like that to children. I was just a child. I loved you.

You abused that and me. I would kill anyone who touched my girls, but you were my father and you did it to me and let Rose do it, too.'

There was silence in the room. Rose still said nothing, she just kept looking at the floor. Never once did she make eye contact with me. I heard the sound of Chris rattling cups in the kitchen and a tiny cry from Carol upstairs in her cot. I just sat there looking at the father I had worshipped as a child and from whom even now I could not entirely detach myself.

He looked at me, he looked at Rose, but she avoided his gaze as well. He fidgeted in his seat, took a number of quick breaths and looked shifty. Then he stood up. His voice was angry, his stance defensive. 'Well, if you're going to just remember things from the past and bring them up like that—'

'Dad,' I interrupted him, 'I just want to know. I need to know. You ruined my life, you raped me. I was just a child.'

He exploded but he didn't make a move towards me. 'If you're going to bring up all that stuff – well, you're no bloody daughter of mine. I don't want to know. I'm not standing here and listening to this fucking rubbish. Things like that happen. They just do, all right?'

I shook my head and he glared at me before turning on his heel and walking out of the house. Rose followed closely behind him. She still hadn't uttered a word. I didn't try to stop them. I just sat there quietly. Tears filled my eyes but I didn't shed them. I remembered all the hurt and all the pain and all the love I had once felt for him, and still I was no closer to knowing why.

A few months later my father called at the house one evening. He said he was just passing but I knew it wasn't true – my house isn't on the way to or from anywhere. He behaved as if nothing had happened, as if he had seen me only the day before and we were on friendly terms.

'I thought I'd pop in and see how the kids were. I haven't seen them for a while. How are my lovely grandchildren, then?'

I said nothing but let him into the house. I was slightly fazed by both his sudden appearance and his attitude.

'I didn't tell your mum I was coming. I just thought I would. OK?'

That was the only reference he made to the fact that things weren't quite right. Then he carried on as if it were a normal family visit.

I spent months considering the situation, but in the end I decided I was the one who was out of step and behaving strangely. This was my family and I shouldn't cut them off. I reverted to the method of dealing with them I had adopted as a child: I accepted the way things were and adapted my own behaviour accordingly to please everyone else. But I never left my father or stepmother alone with my daughters for an instant.

As the whole world now knows, we were not a normal family, but I tried as hard as I could to keep some sort of contact with my father, Rose and my many siblings. I felt my daughters should know their uncles and aunts and occasional family gatherings were an excuse to make sure that my young brothers and sisters were all right. Despite my upbringing I have always had a very strong sense of family and because, after Charmaine had gone, I was the eldest I felt in some ways responsible for the younger children. I have always tried to remember their birthdays and to be there for them if they needed me. But like me they were brainwashed into never going to anyone outside Cromwell Street for help.

Mae and Stephen would sometimes visit me, but if I wanted to see the others I had to go to Cromwell Street. Rose made it clear that just dropping in wasn't acceptable, so I would telephone and ask if it was all right to visit. It was a futile exercise. I was never left alone with any of the younger children, even for a second. They would be very quiet and mostly disappear to their rooms while I was there. If I turned up when Rose wasn't about and Dad was out, the children would turn me away at the gate as they had been instructed to do by their mother. It was more than their lives were worth to go against her. So, just as I had done at their age, they obeyed and survived.

My own survival is something I have questioned time and time again. The police have, too. When dad was first arrested I could tell that the detectives questioning me were convinced I must have been involved in some way — why else would I still be alive? But in time they came to realise, as I did, that it had been a matter of timing. If I hadn't run away when I did, and kept well away for a number of years, then I too would have vanished. I'm sure Rose would have found an excuse for my disappearance, like she did with Charmaine and Heather. But once I had a husband and a family of my own, it was not so easy.

In the early days I think my character kept me alive. Unlike rebellious Charmaine I didn't argue and never spoke up for myself. From a very early age I withdrew into myself and simply accepted everything that happened to me. I was a silent wide-eyed waif who would do as instructed and remained mute much of the time. I was so under Fred and Rose's control that I truly believe they thought I would never tell — and they were right. I kept the dark secrets of Cromwell Street for most of my life. I told my husband a little of what had happened to me, and I revealed some of it to Phil. But to tell everything seemed impossible — it was all so unbelievable.

The police think I was useful to Rose while I was still under her thumb. I was an unpaid skivvy, a built-in housemaid, nanny and sex slave. I wasn't her daughter and she felt nothing for me. I freed up her time so that she could do as she wanted. I had little contact with the outside world and posed no threat to hers.

My father's reasons for wanting me alive were probably more complex. I'm not a psychiatrist and can't pretend to understand them fully. Although it sounds sick in the light of everything that we know now, he *was* genuinely fond of me when I was little. Where the rape when I was just eight fits into that, I don't know. But I was always his favourite; he used to tell me he loved me when I was a kid and as he was all I had, I loved him back. When I was a little older and he was having sex with me regularly he didn't treat me as his daughter but more as his girlfriend. He would tell me after the act of incest that he loved me. God help me, I hated it, but it was the only affection I ever received in my life. I let it continue to please him — and in any case I couldn't have stopped him if I'd tried or had known how to — and because even then I suspected deep down that to resist would bring an even more terrible punishment.

I was devoted to my father, and I know that people will find that almost impossible to understand. I'm not sure I do myself. What he did to me and to others sickens me, but still I went to see him in prison and sent him gifts. Rose had abandoned him, the rest of the family were laying the blame squarely on his shoulders and proclaiming Rose's innocence, and we were back to square one. I was all he had left and it worked both ways.

17

The Ones That Got Away

I don't suppose anyone will ever know how many deaths my father and Rose were responsible for. The police found twelve bodies but there must be families whose daughters remain on a missing persons file who will always wonder. The newspapers were full of stories about how many killings my father admitted to – the estimates ranged from eighteen to sixty. But we will never know now: he took that secret to the grave, and Rose isn't about to tell, either. Dad never told me. Even when he was in prison and rambling on about his past, he never gave much away. As the bodies came out of Cromwell Street one by one I would feel colder, more sick and eventually just more numb. It seemed impossible to take in.

I didn't really know the victims apart from those from my own family and Shirley Robinson. She was nice and took me ice skating, so I remember her better than the others. Sometimes I would walk down to the unemployment office with her. She was a bubbly girl and I spent quite a lot of time talking to her. I would sit in her room and chat.

It was common knowledge that Shirley was having sex with my father and expecting his baby. They would make comments about how she was going to be his next wife. My father liked the fact that Rose and Shirley were fighting for his affections, but it caused tension in the house. Even though she was almost one of the family I didn't really miss her when she disappeared: she was just another transient member of the household.

Just as we will never knowhow many people Fred killed, we might never know how many got away. When the names West and Cromwell Street hit the headlines there must have been a number of women out there forced to relive some sickening incidents they thought they had banished from their minds for good, just like me. I was one of those who got away, the member of the family who probably suffered most but who survived. But there were other women, too, who lived to tell the tale of the dark, depraved world of 25 Cromwell Street. Some of them were brave enough to come forward and tell the police about the horrors they had experienced at the hands of Fred and Rose. It must have cost them a lot, I know. They must have had to tell their families things they had kept secret for years and to relieve them time and time again, first for police statements and then at the trial. Just like me. I admire them for their courage and feel for them deeply. Stepping out of the shadows like that brings you to the very edge of sanity.

There is one particular witness whose evidence affected me deeply. She was named only as Miss A, and her story, to which I referred earlier, still hangs over me like a big black cloud. You see, I was probably there when she was raped but I simply

An aerial shot of Cromwell Street during the excavation work (main) (inset) Police digging in the garden at Cromwell Street
© *Express Newspapers*

(above) My sister Heather, (left) my father and sister Mae (right) in the garden of my home the last time I saw Heather

My stepmother Rose at my daughter's birthday party, days before Heather vanished

(opposite top) At my mother, Catherine Costello's funeral
© *Daily Star*

(opposite) This picture was taken not long after I heard that my father had died
© *Express Newspapers*

Rose is escorted from Gloucester Magistrate's Court
© *South West News*

(below and left) 25 Cromwell Street as it looks today

Police removing the remains of one tragic victim from 25 Cromwell Street
© *Express Newspapers*

Detective Superintendent John Bennett who led the Cromwell Street investigation
© *South West News*

Lucy Katherine Partington (left)
© *South West News*

Shirley Hubbard (right)
© *Popperfoto/Reuters*

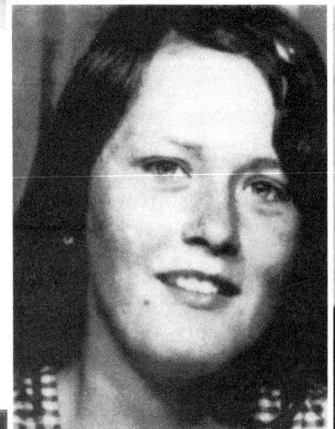

Carol Ann Cooper
© *Popperfoto/Reuters*

Heather West
© *South West News*

Shirley Ann Robinson
© *Popperfoto/Reuters*

Alison Chambers
© *Popperfoto/Reuters*

The twelve young victims. Most of the bodies were found at 25 Cromwell Street (this page and opposite)

Therese Siegenthaler (left)
© *PA News Ltd.*

Catherine Costello (right)
© *PA News Ltd.*

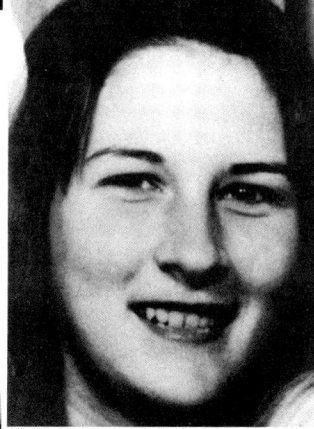

Juanita Mott
© *PA News Ltd.*

Charmaine West
© *South West News*

Anne McFall
© *Popperfoto/Reuters*

Lynda Carole Gough
© *Popperfoto/Reuters*

Out of the Shadows with an eye on the future
© *Express Newspapers*

don't remember. Whether I was drugged at the time or have just blanked it out I don't know. Miss A was thirteen years old when she was placed in care after her parents split up. A friend she made at the children's home took her to Cromwell Street to meet Rose. She found my stepmother kind and caring and was told it was open house, she could visit whenever she wished, particularly if she wanted a shoulder to cry on.

When Miss A was fifteen she ran away from the Jordansbrook home in Gloucester and, having visited Cromwell Street on many occasions, eventually turned up there. Years later she told the police she arrived at about 11 p.m. one night in 1977. She found Rose wearing just a bra and pants. Miss A told Rose that she had run away and poured out her heart. At first Rose comforted her in a motherly fashion and put an arm around her. But then she began to make sexual advances to the girl, which were resisted. Eventually Miss A was given a hot drink and a blanket and spent the night at the house. She was found by her father soon afterwards and returned to the children's home, but she continued to visit Cromwell Street from time to time.

One Friday morning she called there on the way to visit her mother, who lived just outside Gloucester. Rose was in the lounge, wearing a see-through blouse with no bra and a skirt but no tights. She shouted to Fred that Miss A had turned up and followed the girl to the bathroom. Miss A told the police that Rose invited her into one of the bedrooms, where she said there were a couple of visitors of about her age. 'I was stunned to see two naked girls in the room, one on the floor and one on the bed. Fred was there, too,' she Miss A in a statement. She described the first girl as aged about fourteen, 5ft tall with bleached blonde hair, a small bust and painted toenails. The second girl was sitting on the floor and looked older maybe fifteen or sixteen. She seemed quite comfortable and relaxed. She had jet-black hair cut in a short, spiky style, a well-developed bust and an Indian ink tattoo on her wrist. It could only have been me – I drew the tattoo myself at school. Yet I have no recollection of the events that followed.

Miss A, who said she had been sexually abused as a child but had never told anyone, recounted that Rose put an arm around her and said, 'It's all right to touch, to feel, enjoy, and show affection.' Rose then stripped the girl of her clothes and joked: 'It's all girls together.' But Fred was still in the room, sitting there and watching silently. Rose removed her own skirt and blouse and turned to the girl on the bed, who struggled. Rose was calming her down but at the same time touching her breasts and pubic region.

Miss A watched as the girl's hands were bound with wide sticky tape and she was turned on to her stomach by Fred and Rose. 'Rose was reassuring us but Fred was silent. He spread the girl's legs apart and taped her ankles. Her legs were so far apart he almost split her.' Rose then produced a vibrator, a white candle and some ointment and ran the vibrator along the girl's back. She turned to Fred and asked: 'Are you enjoying this now?' before inserting the vibrator into the girl, whose face scrunched up with pain.

Fred had an erection. He knelt behind the girl, raised her buttocks off the bed and had intercourse with her from behind. While this went on Rose stood behind Fred, fondling his backside. Miss A said: 'I looked at the girl's face. She was in pain. She had a help-me look on her face.' The other girl in the room was apparently taking the whole scene in her stride and not reacting. Rose untaped the ankles of the girl on the bed, tearing at the tape to cause maximum pain.

When Miss A made her first statement to the police, she described how she had grabbed her own clothes and run from the house. Later, however, she made another statement detailing what had really happened next. She had gone to the bathroom again and Rose had followed her. I'll let Miss A fell her story in her own words.

I was naked. I froze in fear. She started running her hands across my body and through my public hair. She was also necking me and whispering 'Enjoy, it's all right.'

I never encouraged or welcomed it. I remained frozen in fear. Rose led me to the bed, where the other girl was seated. The dark girl was sitting on the floor with her legs drawn up to her chest. I sat on the bed. Rose got the tape. It was the same as before. Rose put the tape on. I can't understand why I let them do it. She wrapped the tape around my wrists similar to the way bandages go. The other girl got off the bed and leaned against the wall. She looked terrified.

Rose was very aggressive. Fred stood to the right of the bed masturbating himself. I put my head down on the sheets. Rose taped my ankles so they were apart. I couldn't move them.

Something moved down my back. It was cold, hard and vibrating. Rose stood by my left leg. The vibrator got close and was then taken away. She said, 'Is that nice, Fred?' and Fred groaned in reply. I felt Rose push two fingers in my vagina. I know it was Rose. She reached around my body and twisted my left nipple hard. I kept saying to myself, why? She kept saying 'Enjoy.' She called to the other girl and said it was great.

I felt something enter my anus. It was cold, about five or six inches in length and moved forwards and back. There was no lubricant. I felt my anus was being split. I think it was the candle. It was the right dimensions. I assumed it was Rose. It was in place for several minutes and then yanked out very fiercely.

Someone climbed on the bed. I was entered in the vagina. He was moving in and out of me. Rose was fondling Fred as he was having sexual intercourse with me. Fred was telling Rose how close he was to coming. Rose said to come over my back. I felt warm droplets on my back and Rose rubbed it in.

Miss A told the police that someone went out of the room and she was left tied up for some minutes before somebody else cut the tapes with nail scissors and tore them off roughly. She went to the bathroom, found she was bleeding and washed herself, dressed and left the house. She said she could not run because she was so sore. She went on to visit her mother but told no one what had happened to her that day. 'I felt so ashamed,' she said in her statement. She still remembered the sound of the tape being ripped off her body and added: 'I am sure if I had offered any resistance I would have come to some harm.'

Miss A was so distressed by the assault that some weeks later she stole a can of petrol and went to Cromwell Street intending to set fire to number 25. She lost her nerve.

Another survivor who told her story to the police was Caroline Owens, the girl Fred and Rose were accused of kidnapping back in 1972. The incident was reported but unfortunately the main charges against them were dropped because Caroline, only a teenager at the time, felt unable to go through the horrors of a rape trial. Instead Fred and Rose were fined just £50 for assault. The magistrate was quoted in the local paper as saying he did not think a custodial sentence would be of any benefit.

Caroline was sixteen when she met Fred and Rose while hitching a lift to see her boyfriend. They picked her up on a country road in their Ford Popular. She felt safe because they seemed a quiet married couple and during a sociable chat they offered her a job as live-in nanny to their growing family. Later they met Caroline's mother, who lived in nearby Cinderford. Everything seemed above board, so Caroline took the position for wages of £3 a week.

She lasted for only a couple of months. She later told the police that Rose made her feel uncomfortable. She would run her fingers through Caroline's hair, make personal comments and occasionally walked in when she was in the bath. The teenager was none to keen on Fred, either. He made wild claims about having performed abortions on women. Some weeks after she left Cromwell Street Fred and Rose stopped to offer Caroline a lift. As she knew them, she got into the car. Rose put an arm around her with a sinister grin and Fred asked if she had had sex with her boyfriend that evening. Rose began to fondle her breasts and then put a hand between her legs. Fred asked: 'What's her tits like?'

He stopped the car in front of a gateway and Caroline began to struggle with Rose. Fred turned and punched her in the face several times. One blow caught her in the mouth and she blacked out. When she came round Rose and Fred were tying her hands behind her back. Then some kind of tape was wrapped around her face, covering her mouth. In her 1994 statement Caroline told the police: 'I was terrified and crying. My face hurt. I didn't know what was going to happen.'

She was taken back to a first-floor bedroom at 25 Cromwell Street. Using a knife, Fred cut the tape away from her face and untied her hands. She was stripped naked and pushed on to the bed. Rose began to touch her and Fred tied her hands behind her back. The most sickening assault followed. Both Fred and Rose inserted fingers into her vagina. Fred said she was big inside but the outer lips were too fat and hid her clitoris.

> At this stage I was more terrified than I could describe. I thought he was going to do an operation on me. I saw Fred with a leather belt in his hand. Rose held my legs apart. Fred hit me on the vagina with the buckle. He said it would flatten my vaginal lips and I would enjoy sex more. The pain was terrible.
>
> Rose committed oral sex on me. Fred knelt behind Rose and had sex with her from behind. It seemed like a lifetime. I suppose it was just ten minutes.

Next Fred had sex with the terrified girl. He told her he would keep her in his cellar so that his black friends could use her. Then he told her he would kill her and bury her under the paving stones of Gloucester. 'I was in fear of my life and didn't think I would see my mother again,' said Caroline in her statement. 'I was kept there all night. Rose put a pillow over my face. During the night Fred and Rose alternated between being cruel and kind.'

Caroline escaped the next day after agreeing to say nothing and promising that she would return to the house for more. But she didn't — she went to the police, and Fred and Rose were arrested, only to escape full justice because the traumatised girl felt unable to undergo a further ordeal in court.

Out of the Shadows

Another woman was able to give the police a terrifying insight into the sexual behaviour of Fred and Rose. She came forward following my father's arrest and described in detail her association with the killers of Cromwell Street. She too must have felt lucky to be alive, for she had at first taken part willingly in their bizarre sex games, only to become trapped in a web of fear, lust, and violence.

Divorcee Catherine Mary Halliday, who was bisexual, left her husband and moved into a rented flat in Cromwell Street with a woman friend in October 1988. She met my father when he went to mend a leak in the roof at her flat, and he invited her to number 25 for a drink.

Catherine told the police that they went to the upstairs living room, where she noticed a unit full of video cassettes. Fred asked her what she wanted to watch and she told him a straight blue movie. He selected one and put it on. A woman entered the room. She was wearing a very short skirt and a low-cut short-sleeved top. It was obvious she was not wearing any underwear. Within minutes Rose had removed what few clothes she was wearing and was naked on the settee alongside Catherine. Catherine's statement read:

> Rose removed all my clothes. I was dragged rather than led to the bedroom. Fred followed behind with the drinks. He was still fully clothed. Rose started to make love to me. Fred was in the room and took his clothes off. He was naked and he had a video camera.
>
> 'I felt Rose was getting me excited in preparation for Fred. After a short period Fred joined us on the bed and had sex with me. While Fred was making love to me I was still stimulating Rose.

She said that after Fred climaxed Rose's behaviour changed. 'She became the aggressor . . . she became more violent . . . more menacing . . . more abusive with my body.'

The sex session went on until 3 a.m., and after that Catherine Halliday became a regular visitor to 25 Cromwell Street. She went most mornings when the children had left the house and had sex with Rose. Rose, she said, liked to use large sex aids. There were evening visits, too, when she would have sex with both Fred and Rose.

On one occasion they took her to their back bedroom, where they had a large homemade four-poster bed. There were two large metal hooks in the wooden pelmet. In the wardrobe were two whips, a bullwhip and a cat-o'-nine-tails. Fred showed her a catalogue offering rubber clothing, including latex suits which covered the eyes and head. Some had nose holes, others didn't. Then he took out a suitcase containing similar outfits, all black. 'He took out one suit but it smelled sweaty and had been worn. He wanted me to put it on but I refused,' said Catherine. Rose, too, showed her a collection of sexy clothes.

Catherine Halliday told the police she had regular three-in-a-bed sessions with Rose and Fred and was often tied to the bed and tormented by the couple. 'I felt on each occasion they were trying to take me to my physical and emotional limit. There was verbal abuse during the sex act about my inability to accept into my body the larger sex aids which Rose accepted more readily.'

In a second statement she told of seeing a terrifying porno movie which had obviously been filmed at the house. It showed a young woman tied to a bed and spreadeagled on her back. She was being abused with a large sex aid and the camera operator concentrated on her obvious distress. Catherine also saw a number of other movies at Cromwell Street, featuring bondage, rubber masks and chains. She added:

> What I didn't describe in my previous statement was the sheer terror and life-threatening situations Fred and Rose led me into — nor did I give details of the full abuse. They became more and more violent, physically and mentally. Fred would beat me around the head with his fists and Rose slapped me.
> Each time they pushed me a little further. On numerous occasions I was tied up and blindfolded. Rose would lie across my face and they would put a pillow over my face so I couldn't breathe. On one occasion they threatened to cut my throat or stomach. I could feel cold metal on my stomach. Afterwards I found a half-inch cut close to my belly button, although it wasn't deep. I was so frightened I never went back.

My father and stepmother often tried to interest neighbours and family in their sexual games. Fred thought nothing of talking dirty to anyone he imagined might be interested. After their arrest it wasn't just those who succumbed who went to the police. People who, back then, dismissed their tales as fantasy were also able to throw light on the activities of the West household.

Mrs Elizabeth Agius, who was married to a Maltese man and had two young children, got to know Dad and Rose when she moved into the house next door to us in Midland Road. It was the autumn of 1971, when I was six years old. She told detectives she first met Fred when he offered to help her with her pram as she struggled down some steps. Later he invited her in for a cup of tea and she met Rose. Mrs Agius said Rose only looked about fourteen and was obviously pregnant. Her new-found friends questioned her closely about her own personal life and she began to visit them quite regularly in a neighbourly way.

Fred once helped her decorate a room. She said in a statement: 'That was the sort of person he was, always helpful if he could be. He was a real sweet talker. He would charm most women, a real gentleman.' Mrs Agius first became aware of the Wests' unusual sex life when Rose told her that Fred wanted her to join them in a three-in-a-bed session.

> She said Fred was falling in love with me and desperate to have sex with me. She did her best to encourage me. One day she took me into the bedroom and took out two boxes. There were tablets, coloured capsules, she said she used for protection against disease when having sex. She told me she had sex with other men. There were condoms and rubber things. I told her I wasn't interested. She told me she liked Fred to watch her having sex and there was a hole in the wall. If Fred wasn't there she had to tell him all about it.

Mrs Agius told the police that by the time she had known the couple about nine months Fred's remarks were starting to get more suggestive. He told her he would like to tie her to the bed; he said she could burn him with a cigarette or whip him. He would make the comments in front of Rose. 'I used to laugh it off,' she said.

One day the couple revealed how they often played out their favourite fantasy. They told their astonished neighbour that they went looking for young female hitch-hikers. Fred claimed he got them into prostitution. He liked them to be between fifteen and seventeen years old because they were more likely to be virgins and you could get more money for virgins.

In her statement Mrs Agius said the Wests told her it was easier to get the girls into the car with Rose present. Often the girls had run away from home and had no money and would do anything for cash and a place to live. She said: 'I babysat when they were out. Once they came back very late. It was in the early hours of the morning. They had been as far as London looking. Fred said the best pick-up place was Bristol, because there were a lot of young girls trying to get to the bright lights of London.'

The relationship between the neighbours changed when Mrs Agius's husband returned home from Malta. She tried to introduce him to Fred. 'Fred got quite funny and stormed off into the kitchen. He said: "I'll kill him and put him down there," indicating the cellar. He said: "If I can't have you, why can he?" I said he was nuts.'

She told, too, of how one day Fred burst in while she was chatting with Rose and disappeared into a bedroom. When he emerged he grabbed her by the left arm and snapped a pair of handcuffs on her wrist. He said: 'Now I've fucking got you.' Rose told him to take them off and he complied.

When the Wests announced that they were moving to Cromwell Street Fred asked the young neighbour to take a room there with him. But she again laughed off his suggestion. What he told her next was ominous. He was thinking, he said, of converting the cellar of the new house into a children's playroom. But then he added: 'I could soundproof it and make it my torture chamber.'

* * *

It's hard to say how many people knew what was going on or had their suspicions. During the 1980s, after I had left home, it seems that my father and stepmother were even more open about their perversions. Men called at the house regularly for Rose and she was even advertising her services locally. Fred, meanwhile, was becoming known for his home movies.

Rose's brother Graham Letts and sister-in-law Barbara told newspaper reporters how they found out about the sick goings-on at 25 Cromwell Street. From their experience, it seems they were hardly hidden from visitors. Barbara said:

> It was obvious that Fred had an abnormal sex drive. As time went on it got more and more out of control. If we stayed for any length of time he and Rose would have to disappear upstairs for sex. They were quite open about it. One time they showed me a blue bottle which had been sealed. Inside was a pair of Rosemary's knickers. She said she'd worn them during a fantastic sex session with Fred. She wanted to preserve them as a souvenir.

Barbara and Graham felt that Fred and Rose were trying to draw them into their sordid world. They were invited to see the top floor of the house and discovered that it was decorated with framed pictures of Rose in the nude. There was a huge library of porno videos, including some involving animals. When Rose put one on for them to watch the Letts walked out.

> Another time we were sitting downstairs when Rose suddenly announced that she wanted to change her

clothes. There and then she stripped right off. She wasn't wearing knickers — I don't think she ever did. I didn't know where to look. It was awful. I think it was her way of trying to initiate us into their world.

Graham Letts once tackled his sister after hearing rumours that she was operating as a prostitute. She confessed immediately.

What shocked me most was how casual she was about the whole thing. She and Fred seemed to take pride in how slick the operation was. I was stunned, but Rose said I was overreacting.
    Quite often we'd be there and the phone would go and Rosie would have to disappear for half an hour. But if I had known just how much deeper their perversions went I would have blown the whistle.

18

The Day My Father Died

On 31 December 1994 I sat at home with my family and friends and toasted the old year out and the new one in. I knew I still had to face the trial, but I felt that whatever 1995 brought it couldn't be as bad as 1994. I looked at the people around me – my daughter Carol (Michelle was with her father) my partner and friend Phil, his family, and others who had stuck by me – and thanked God for their constant support. The nightmare wasn't over, but they made it easier to bear.

I looked out of the window into the dark, depressing street and raised my glass of sparkling wine in a silent toast to my mother and sisters Charmaine and Heather. I wanted them to know they would live on in my memory and my heart forever and that soon I would be putting them to rest. I was quiet for a while as I thought about how much I missed them and how much I would have liked them to have been there with us then. The Christmas tree lights twinkled, the fire glowed, the walls and ceiling were covered in festive decorations. It was a normal family scene, duplicated all over the country, but there were too many people missing from our house.

I snapped out of my morbid mood for the sake of the others, casting a wry, sad look at Phil and getting a supportive, affectionate nod in return, and carried on socialising and amusing my daughter. Christmas was the same to her this year as any other – I made sure of that. She had lots of presents and plenty of attention. Michelle was spending the holiday with her father from choice, which caused me heartache, but she was not left out.

New Year's Day was spent visiting relatives and friends. I can't honestly say I started 1995 with a new spring in my step or in a particularly optimistic mood, but there was a feeling of new beginnings in the air and the hope that by the end of it all everything might be dealt with and I would be free to start again. Nothing had prepared me for the announcement that was to come at four o'clock that afternoon.

I did not see the television or hear the radio because we were at a friend's house. We didn't have the radio on in the car going home either. So while the rest of the world knew that my father was dead and all over the country the media went into a feeding frenzy, it was another two hours before the news got through to me.

The police informed the press that all Fred West's next of kin had been notified of his death, but they hadn't. I was told in a telephone call from a relative on my mother's side. I couldn't take in what she was saying as I stood in my little narrow hallway clutching the receiver.

'He's dead. It's all on the news. He's hanged himself.'

'Who?'

'Your bloody father. There'll be no trial now. He's done us all a favour.'

I stopped breathing. My mouth was dry. I let out a cry of pure anguish and dropped the phone. I ran into the other room, hysterical. I sounded and felt like a wounded animal. All the hurt crashed and exploded inside me and it was more than I could bear. Phil came running, took one look at the dropped receiver, picked it up and yelled: 'Who the hell is this upsetting Anne? What have you said to her? How dare you do this!'

He fell silent as the voice at the other end began to explain what happened. 'OK. I'm sorry. Of course she had to know, but you should have done it more gently or spoken to me first . . . Of course she's upset. Yes, she knows what he did. But he was still her father, for God's sake.'

The conversation was cut short and Phil came back into the room and put his arms around me. I sobbed hysterically for I don't know how long. I was in such a state I could barely catch my breath. I didn't know what I was feeling except pain, hurt and anger. Would it never end?

I don't really drink much but I had had a glass earlier in the day to be sociable and now I had another and another. I had already taken the drugs prescribed by my doctor but I forgot and took them again. I didn't want to kill myself, just the pain. I drank a mixture of spirits that night and my head hurt even more so I took more tablets. The telephone didn't stop ringing and the sound jarred my brain. Phil persuaded me to lie down for a while but I couldn't settle. They called my doctor but nothing anybody did or said could take away the screaming in my head. I insisted on going to see my father's brother Doug and his wife Christine, who live in Much Marcle, my father's home village. Everyone tried to change my mind, but eventually Phil had to give in and take me there. I don't know why I wanted to go, I just did.

When we arrived Christine gave me another drink. I knocked it back without thinking. I wasn't making much sense to anybody. I just kept repeating, 'I'm sorry, I'm sorry,' but I didn't know what for and neither did they. I was slurring my words by then and must have appeared completely drunk, but it was a combination of tablets, booze and grief. The tears wouldn't stop; even when I was more calm they still streamed down my face. Eventually Phil talked me into going home. I got into the car and curled up in the front passenger seat, a heap of lonely misery.

The events that followed are, not surprisingly, something of a blur. I must have taken more tablets when we got home and at some point Phil realised that I wasn't just drunk but had reached danger level. There was a mad dash to Gloucester Hospital in his car and the humiliation and pain of having my stomach pumped. I was still hysterical and kept refusing treatment. I tried to discharge myself and insisted I wouldn't agree to anything unless I could talk to Nick Barnes the detective constable assigned to me who had taken all my statements. Phil managed to find him and he came at once.

The hospital psychiatrist didn't want me released and threatened to have me committed, but later my doctor's wife, also a psychiatrist there, agreed that I would be better off at home. I was desperate to get back to my daughter and to reassure her that I was all right and I would have fought anybody who tried to stop me.

The police took me home. I was pale, washed out and full of shame. I couldn't believe what I had done. I felt so stupid. Everyone said it was a cry for help, but it wasn't even that. I was just so confused that I didn't know what I had taken or what I had had to drink. I certainly hadn't meant to harm myself. I wouldn't have done that — I had my girls to think of. I would never leave them.

Two days later some of the newspapers got hold of the story through one of my relatives. The headlines read: 'NOW WEST GIRL TRIES TO KILL HERSELF.' Meanwhile the *Daily Star* told of my accidental overdose. Their version is right, I promise you. No matter how low I have got since all this happened I would never abandon my daughters. The day I came home from the hospital Carol looked at me gravely and said: 'I don't want you to go away or die, Mummy, because I love you. You won't, will you?'

'No, darling, I won't,' I told her with a hug, tears welling up once again. But I blinked them back, knowing that reassuring her would make me stronger too.

I know many people did not understand how I could be upset by my father's death. It was partly shock, of course, and the way it happened. Fred hanged himself with a sheet in his cell at Winson Green Prison in Birmingham, where he had been on remand almost since his arrest. Warders tried to revive him, but it was too late.

I had been visiting Dad at Winson Green on and off over the months and he regularly telephoned me. He had a cell to himself and every opportunity to do himself harm if he wanted to. On one of my last visits he had talked about taking his own life and I became concerned that he might mean to do it. I told the police and they in turn informed the prison authorities. Dad was put on a special watch, where by they checked him every fifteen minutes, but his behaviour seemed normal and after a while they went back to checking on him at the same intervals as other prisoners.

The day Dad told me he wanted to end his own life he

cried for a long time. We sat in the depressing visitors' room and he talked about arrangements for his funeral and what he wanted done with his things. He had his elbows on the table between us and he leaned forward as he spoke to me. 'I've told them here I want you down as my next of kin. Rose don't want me no more. She don't want to know.'

I bit my lip. I didn't want this conversation. 'Dad, don't. Don't talk about it.'

'No, I want to. I've told them my girl is next of kin. She'll sort things out. Your dad's had enough, love. I'm going to finish it myself. I've had enough.'

'Dad, don't talk like this. You'll be all right. You don't want to do anything like that. Don't be silly.'

He was crying as he told me, 'I want to be buried with your mum. I want to be with her. I don't want to be on my own. And I want Charmaine there too. Put me with them, love. You'll see to it, won't you?'

I was stunned, horrified. I just stared at him. He reached across the table and stroked the side of my face and then he took my hand. 'I want you buried there too one day. With me.'

I pulled my hand back. A shiver ran down my spine. 'No, Dad. It's not right. You can't do that and I won't do it for you. You can't be buried with Mum and Charmaine. Think of Mum's family. There's been too much hurt already.'

I could see that he wasn't taking in what I was saying. He had made up his mind that that was what he wanted and he really thought I would do it. He was still crying, but he didn't say much more about it. He looked really depressed when I left and I was convinced then that he might try to kill himself.

Yet earlier during that visit, at the end of November

1994, he had seemed quite cheerful. He asked me what I was doing with his tropical fish, which he had insisted I looked after.

'I'm frying them with chips tonight,' I said. He laughed and seemed quite amused. He told me he wanted me to have a lock of his hair and said that I would have to smuggle it out in my knickers. Then he made a crude joke – the sort of humour dad specialised in, which had always embarrassed the girls in the family.

During that last visit my father also asked me to go and see a woman he knew who, he claimed, would give him an alibi which would help his case. I hated it when he asked me to do things like that. He should have known I wouldn't. 'I can't do that for you, Dad,' I said.

That was when his mood began to change. The humour disappeared and he sounded more morose and depressed. 'Well, I'll get out of here one way or another.'

I attempted to change the subject. 'What would you like for Christmas, Dad?'

He tried to make light of it but there was a lot of feeling behind his reply. 'A helicopter would be nice. Could you smuggle one of them in under your skirt?'

Those visits to Winson Green were always a trial for me. For a start I don't drive, and getting there and back wasn't always easy. When I first started going I had to walk through the crowded visitors' hall to reach him. Everyone would be staring at me; they knew who I was. And then when Dad appeared they would look at him too. We were the cabaret. At the beginning I had to talk to him through a screen. I was taken into a room and locked in and then he would come in through a door on the other side and we spoke to each other through a grille. That was very difficult. It was so hard to communicate on any level with a thick piece of plastic between you.

Later, when Dad had been there a little longer and the prison authorities had obviously decided I wasn't a threat, we were allowed to talk in a small room with just a table between us. I was able to hold Dad's hand and comfort him when he got upset. Those visits never lasted any longer than forty minutes and there were always two or three prison guards in there with us.

Dad often wanted to talk about Anne McFall, the friend of my mother's from Scotland whose body was found in Much Marcle. I, of course, wanted to talk about my mother. He would tell me time and time again how much he had loved Anne. They had been planning to buy a house together and live there with me and Charmaine.

I asked him: 'And did you love Mum too?'

'No,' he said. 'It was different with your mum.'

He claimed Rena hadn't loved me or Charmaine; that she didn't look after us properly and kept us filthy dirty. I didn't believe him.

Whenever dad talked about Anne McFall he would cry. He said he was going to write a book about her. At first he wanted to write a book about my mum and said he wanted me to help him. 'I don't want anything to do with it, Dad,' I responded. 'You murdered my mum. I can't help you write about her.'

He upset me most when he claimed that my mother had killed Anne. He said he had got home late one night from his job as a delivery driver. It was about 10 p.m. when he reached the Timberland Caravan park in Brockworth, Gloucester, where he had been living with Anne. He said Rena and a black man were there and had killed Anne between them.

He told me they had cut her legs off and were trying to fit the body into a suitcase. They were hysterical and wanted to dump it on a council tip. Fred said he told them that was stupid and they begged him for help, so he took the body to Much Marcle and buried it in Fingerpost Field. I repeated that story to the police but they assured me it was nonsense.

Occasionally he would deny all involvement in the murders and say simply, 'I didn't do it. It wasn't me.'

I would reply: 'Only you know what really happened, Dad.'

He would never go into much detail when he did discuss the murders, but once he did tell me about a ruse Rose had used to ensnare one young girl. She told the teenager she was a seamstress and could make her a dress. When the girl came to the house Rose said: 'I can't fit you for a dress unless you take all your clothes off.'

I don't know who that young girl was, or if she survived.

During those awful prison encounters I felt as if I were visiting someone who was terminally ill. I had lost my dad a long time ago, but I kept going to see the stranger he had become because I didn't want him getting low or depressed. He could explain so much about my life. That was why I kept going back. And I didn't want him to get lonely because I knew what that was like.

The last time I spoke to my father was on the telephone on 22 December 1994, ten days before he died. He asked after his grandchildren and his seven assorted tropical fish, which were now ensconced in a huge tank on a bookshelf in my living room. At the time he sounded very upbeat and happy. I was surprised at that because he was still waiting to be told when the hearing date for the committal proceedings would be. I asked him if would like to talk to Carol. He said, 'Yes, I will speak to the little one.' They chatted for about five minutes and then she put him back on to me. I explained that I was trying to arrange to see him before Christmas to bring him his tobacco, a £20 postal order to buy things from the prison shop and some drawing materials. 'Don't worry about popping up,' he said. 'You can come after Christmas.' He sounded quite full of himself so I sent a parcel instead going myself.

Even so, the end of the conversation left me with an eerie feeling. Dad went very quiet and then murmured, 'Goodbye, my angel,' before hanging up. It felt like the final goodbye. And of course, that is exactly what it was.

The last time I saw him he was laid out on a slab at Birmingham Mortuary. They asked me to identify him as Fred West and I did, but he wasn't the dad I knew, the one I remembered from my early childhood who used to ruffle my hair and tell me he loved me. That moment in that cold, bleak place will stay with me forever. He didn't look at rest or at peace – and I don't suppose he ever will be.

19

Funerals

I thought things couldn't get worse. My father was dead, Rose's solicitor was trumpeting her innocence in the press following the decision at Dursley Magistrates Court to commit her for trial, I was having trouble with my eldest daughter and still hadn't been able to bury my mother and sister because the defence had retained Charmaine's body. There were constant interviews with the police and my stress levels were going through the roof.

I should have known better. Things can always get worse – and they did. On 28 March 1995, nearly three months after my father hanged himself in prison, I got a phone call telling me that my half-brother Stephen and sister Mae had taken his body from the mortuary. No one knew where it was. I was devastated. It wasn't hard to see what they were up to. Stephen and Mae had signed with a Sunday newspaper and sold Dad's funeral as an exclusive.

It wasn't how I planned it. I knew people were asking

questions about why Fred had not yet been buried or cremated, but I had made it clear soon after his death that I wanted all the victims buried first as a sign of respect for the families. Those victims included my own mother and sister. I had no control over when Heather would be laid to rest — I was not her next of kin. That decision fell to Rose and upon her arrest to Stephen and Mae. They had already told me that Heather's funeral would not be held until Rose was free and could attend the service. I felt they would have a very long wait.

I didn't know where to turn. The police were sympathetic and tried to help, but they had no jurisdiction over what happened to my father's remains. They managed to contact Stephen early on and he told them that he wanted me at the funeral but Mae did not (there was friction between us because I had agreed to give evidence at the trial). I might be notified, I might not. Then Stephen and Mae disappeared and even the police were unable to contact them. They had been spirited away by the newspaper. I realised that I was not going to be invited to my own father's funeral. I was very bitter. Mae had said she didn't want anything to do with Dad: she blamed him for everything and believed her mother was innocent. She wouldn't even go and visit her father in prison, but now here she was organising his funeral and excluding me.

I spent most of that day in tears. It all seemed so wrong, so disrespectful to the rest of the family. Even Dad's brothers and sisters were banned from the service and didn't even know where it would be held. I also felt that it was unfair to Mum and Charmaine, and my mother's own family, who were still waiting to say their painful goodbyes.

I was well aware that my father's funeral could turn into a media event and I had taken advice on how to handle it. I wanted a cremation with just the family there and the media presence kept at enough of a distance to allow us to behave with dignity. But as it turned out the ceremony was anything but dignified, as I discovered later from the undertakers who had organised it, the same firm I had booked. They refused to give me any details about where his body was being kept and even denied their involvement until the whole thing was over. I wasn't even given the chance to go to the chapel of rest and say my own private farewell. I know many people will wonder why I would want to, but it was just something I needed to do. It was my way of dealing with what had happened and bringing part of the horror to a close. And I can only repeat that he was my father. Unable to abandon him in life, I couldn't do so in death, either.

The funeral was held the day after it was reported that his body had disappeared from the Birmingham Mortuary. I spoke to everyone I could think of in my attempts to find out where the service was to be held. I was passed from pillar to post as everybody passed the buck and refused to accept responsibility. The coroner's office would only tell me that Stephen, as the eldest son, had a right to take the body and it was no one's responsibility to let me know. No laws had been broken and nobody felt any moral obligation to inform me, even though it was I who had identified Dad's body in the first place and well known that I was dealing with all the arrangements.

So Dad was taken to Coventry Crematorium, several other crematoria around the country having refused to handle the funeral. The Sunday newspaper with which Mae and Stephen were involved tried to cancel the ceremony when they learned that journalists on their own sister paper had found out where the service would be. But it was too late, Dad's body had arrived. The service went ahead like a scene from a black comedy. Photographers leaped around the coffin as it was taken from the hearse. Then just as the curtains were about to close to allow the coffin to disappear from sight, the man from the *Sun* pulled out a sure-shot camera and snapped away. There was a scuffle as the *News of the World* reporters tried to wrest it from him and insults were traded. Crematorium staff were horrified. The only family members there to witness this farce were Stephen, Mae and my seventeen-year-old half-sister. I can't say I was sorry to have missed it.

It was lunchtime before I finally discovered where the cremation was taking place. By then it was too late. The service had been held at 10 a.m. I felt I needed to do something to mark the day, so I arranged with the supervisor at the crematorium to spend a few quiet moments in the chapel where they had had the service. I dressed in the black suit and funeral hat I had planned to wear. I was pale and shaky but determined to go. There were reporters and cameramen all over the place, but they didn't know who I was and I was driven right to the door of the chapel. I sat there quietly with Phil, thinking my own thoughts and shedding a few tears. When I left I took with me a small cutting of the flowers which adorned the chapel altar. It was all that was left.

The service for my mother and Charmaine was very different. I was able to plan it carefully in the way I wanted and with my new-found relatives. Mum's family are Catholic and wanted a ceremony which reflected their beliefs. I am not religious but I was happy to acknowledge their wishes. We decided to have a cremation in Kettering, near my aunts' homes in Corby. Their local priest, Father Peter Wilson, would officiate and one of the local nuns, Sister Stephanie, was to read the lesson.

I chose the hymns and the music. I sent a tape of Andrew Lloyd Webber's hauntingly beautiful song 'Memories' — just the music, not the lyrics — to the crematorium supervisor and asked him to play it as the mourners came in. I wanted everyone to be able to sit and think of their own memories of Mum and Charmaine for a few moments. I knew the music was sad and emotional and might make us cry, but I didn't mind that. I felt that for every tear we shed a little bit of us, Mum's family, would go with her that day.

It was an unusual request, but I also requested that Mum and Charmaine shared the same coffin. My sister had missed her mother so much and wanted so much to be with her. Charmaine was always the one Mum doted on, too. My father and Rose had separated them in life; now I could reunite them in death. I sent a cross of pink carnations to be placed on the coffin for my mother and a posy of spring flowers for Charmaine. I gave strict instructions that there were to be no roses at the funeral from anybody. I wanted no reminder of my stepmother on this of all days. The flowers I sent were to be burned with the coffin. I wrote the messages on the accompanying cards myself, the same words I had written when I placed flowers at Midland Road for Charmaine and in the windswept, deserted Much Marcle field for my mother.

Choosing the hymns was difficult. As I said, I am not religious, but I still wanted it to be right and I wanted to demonstrate some of the confused emotions I was feeling. My aunts wanted 'Amazing Grace' and I was pleased with that. I spent some time trying to find something which expressed my own feelings. Eventually I found what I wanted. It is a prayer as well as a hymn and comes from Isaiah 43, i–iv. It was read as part of the lesson and then sung by the congregation. The chorus goes:

> Do not be afraid for I have redeemed you. I have called you by your name; You are mine.

The verses which moved me to tears said:

> When you walk through the waters, I'll be with you,
> You will never sink beneath the waves.
> When the fire is burning all around you,
> You will never be consumed by the flames.
> When the fear of loneliness is looming,
> Then remember I am at your side.
> When you dwell in exile like the stranger,
> Remember you are precious in my eyes.

I bought a new black hat for the funeral – I did not want to wear the one I had chosen for Dad's. I felt quite strong during the service. One of my aunts collapsed in sobs at the end, but somehow I managed to keep going. I looked at all the flowers, including a teddy bear of blooms for Charmaine from my cousins. I had photographs taken of them so that I would always have a record of the day I said both hello and goodbye to my mother and sister.

The service for mum and Charmaine was well attended. There was a large contingent from Gloucester Police, led by DS John Bennett and including Nick, the detective who had spent so many hours taking my statement. I took only Phil and a woman friend with me. Father Wilson spoke of the tragedy which had brought us all together. He said:

Out of the Shadows

The whole world has heard of the dreadful events that are the reason for our being here. Through the media the names Rena and Charmaine are well known. To most people they remain just that. But to those here today they are family, they are friends, who have been wondered about, worried about and prayed for during the many years of uncertainty and they have been deeply mourned when the fact and manner of their death became known.

He said only time would help the family pray for God's forgiveness for those who did them hurt.

The prayer read by my cousins ran:

We pray for Anna-Marie, who mourns the loss of her mother and sister today. May she feel the love and support of her mum's family that surrounds her at this time.

We pray for all our family and friends, that the healing touch of God may bring us peace.

The Lord said: 'Do not be afraid, for I am with you.' We pray that these words will be a source of strength, support and comfort at this troubled time.

We pray that today we may realise deep in our hearts that God has called Aunt Rena and Charmaine to life in his Kingdom of eternal love, where no more sadness or suffering can touch them. Lord hear us.

I mingled with my mother's family in the brilliant, hot spring sunshine and had the opportunity to meet one of her oldest friends. The setting was beautiful. The crematorium had sweeping green lawns and flowers everywhere. I felt a certain amount of peace in spite of my raw emotions. I rode with the family in the big black funeral car back to my aunt's house in Corby and tried my best to keep going. I stayed only a short time. The family were very kind that day, but it was still difficult for me to be at ease with them. No one wanted my father's name mentioned, of course, but I was still his daughter as well as Rena's. I think everyone's emotions were confused. No doubt my aunts will spend the rest of their lives wondering if there was something they could have done all those years ago. But the family had cut her off in disgrace and no amount of wishing can change things.

I left the house as soon as was polite and went back to the crematorium to collect my mother's and sister's ashes. They had placed them in a traditional urn for me. I took it home and placed it in the living room. It might seem macabre to some, but I wanted to have Mum and Charmaine at home with me, at least for a little while. Eventually I would decide what to do with the ashes, perhaps take them back to Scotland, my mother's home, and scatter them there. But I did not want to make any decisions until the whole ordeal of Rose's trial was out of the way.

When it was all over and I was on my way home I felt drained but strangely satisfied and relieved. At last I had been able to close one chapter of my life with dignity. The mother and sister I thought had abandoned me were now with me again and at rest.

It was so different and so much more comforting than the first time I had been reunited with my mother in that desolate field in Much Marcle in April 1994. All that remained for me to see that day was the bare earth which had covered my mum's body in a corner of Letterbox Field, the spot where she had spent her courting days with Dad.

The day I made my pilgrimage was cold and wet and my tears mingled with the rain as I looked down into the clay pit where my mother had lain for over twenty-five years. The police had taken me there in an unmarked car after I insisted on seeing what had become of the woman who gave me life.

There was a lot of police activity when we arrived and a few curious sightseers. I felt cold and numb. A tarpaulin surrounded a small area of one corner of the field and I had to summon the strength to approach it. It wasn't easy, but by then I was beginning to find courage I never knew I possessed. After a few seconds I took a deep breath and, clutching Phil's hand, nodded to the detective escorting us. We were led over to the spot where the earth had been disturbed. There were wooden boards covering the hole they had excavated. One of the police officers involved in the dig asked me if I wanted the boards removed. I shook my head. I didn't want to look down into that godforsaken place. The policemen withdrew tactfully and stood a little way behind us.

I laid the flowers I had brought with me against a lone tree at the corner of the field and fought to control my emotions. The card with the flowers said everything I wanted to say: 'To my mum, wanting, missing, hurting and needing you so very much. Will always love and remember you.'

We stood quietly by the tree for a few moments. It was impossible to stand any nearer because the hole in the earth was so big and it was dangerous. I was shaking and in tears, but not really sobbing. I looked at Phil and asked him: 'How could anybody do this?' He shook his head in sorrowful reply. I gazed at the spot and whispered: 'I'm sorry, Mum, so sorry.'

My nose started to bleed. Phil gave me a handkerchief and I just stood there crying and trying to deal with my bloody nose. After a while one of the detectives came and asked if I was all right. I was only partly aware that we were being videoed by police cameras. They had warned us about this: it was necessary to show that we hadn't interfered with evidence. So, surrounded by onlookers and under the watchful eye of the police, I said my first goodbye in that barren field and thought: 'This is it. This is what became of my mum. She didn't leave me because she didn't love me. She couldn't help it.'

I accepted then I would never see my mother again. There would be no happy reunion like those you see on television. My mum hadn't contacted me because she couldn't. That my father had left her somewhere she had been happy didn't help. Somehow it just made it more cruel.

I gazed across the countryside, which seemed to stretch for miles. The ploughed field was bordered by a small hedgerow which afforded little protection from the wind and driving rain. I wondered what it had been like on a summer's day when it was covered in grass and birds sang and a young woman shared a picnic and romance with a man she thought adored her.

It hurt so much. Over and over in my mind I kept saying: 'I'm so sorry, Mum.' I was sorry I hadn't searched for her in time; sorry because I loved her and she didn't know; sorry because it looked as if I had disowned her when all I had ever really wanted was for us to be together again. I wanted to be able to say: 'Look, Mum, these are my children. Aren't they lovely? They look like you and me, they look like us.' Carol says to me sometimes: 'How old would Nanny be now?' I tell her Nanny is asleep now and happy and with Auntie Charmaine.

Out of the Shadows

We walked back to the car. The field was thick with clay and it was all over my shoes. The policemen were looking at me. I suppose it was curiosity, because then no one knew what I looked like. I just kept my head down, the handkerchief covering my nose, and Phil helped me into the back seat. With great care and affection he put his arm round me and let me sob out my grief. The detectives left us alone for a few moments and then got back in the front and started the engine. The woman officer turned and looked at me. I knew she didn't believe I had no knowledge of my father's crimes. She said 'Any thoughts now, Anne Marie?'

I shook my head and lowered my eyes. Oh, I had thoughts, all right – thoughts of a mother I had waited for for a lifetime, thoughts of a woman I believed had deserted me and longed to know – but I wasn't going to share them with her.

20

Life Now

Throughout recent events life has gone on. I get up in the morning, get breakfast, get the children off to school, go to work as a dinner lady at the same school, make the tea, watch television, go to bed. Sometimes I sleep, mostly I don't. Sometimes I eat the food I cook for the family, mostly I don't. Sometimes I concentrate on the programme I'm watching, mostly I don't.

Since the day Detective Hazel Savage first knocked at my door I have lived in a vacuum, almost like a time warp. I may appear to be functioning normally but I'm just keeping up appearances. At first I could barely cry, then there were days when I could hardly stop. It is hard to describe what goes on in my mind; sometimes nothing, sometimes more than I can cope with.

I have been lucky in having a good GP who, when absolutely necessary, has prescribed what I call my 'happy pills' and occasionally something to help me sleep. But generally I have carried on through my own strength of will and because I have had no choice. I have been offered counselling but decided against it. I don't want to cloud my mind; I want to be clear about what I truly remember. When everything is over and done with, then I will get help. But I resolved quite early on that I would have to be strong until the trial, and that I could be. The police did arrange for me to see a psychologist but I only went once. They hoped it would prompt me to remember things I had blanked out, but I knew after just the one session that it was not for me, at least not yet.

The major part of my life after Dad's arrest was taken up by the police. I couldn't make even short-term plans without consulting them first. I made so many statements I lost count of them, but hardly a week went by when they weren't at my house. At first they were quite tough on me, suspecting that I knew more than I did or had some sort of involvement in the murders. This made me angry. After all, my mother and two sisters were among the victims. I speak my mind and I tell the truth, and after a while a sort of mutual respect developed. Their approach became more sensitive and every questioning session would start in the kitchen with a cup of tea.

I began to unburden my memory, and despite the years the detectives had spent in the force, I think even they were shocked at some of the things I had to tell them. Hours, days and weeks were taken up making statements, reading them back and signing them. When they had evidence from someone else they came back to me to see if I could confirm the story, and they tried to cross-check everything I told them with the statement of other witnesses. It was an ongoing process almost up until the trial.

Some weeks it got more intense. After Dad killed himself it

Out of the Shadows

felt as though they had moved in. It was only six weeks before he had been due to appear with Rose at Dursley Magistrates Court for committal proceedings to see if there was a case to answer. It was explained to me that there would be, and that this was just a legal tactic by the defence. The run-up to the Dursley proceedings, now involving only Rose, was nerve-racking. The police told me it was likely I would be called to give evidence. None of what I, or the other witnesses, said could be reported due to legal restrictions, but I would still have to stand up there and say it. I was terrified. Rose would be watching me with those evil eyes and the world's press would fill the court.

The detectives assigned to me took me to see the courtroom a week beforehand so that I would know where I was meant to stand and where the magistrate would sit. It made me feel a little more at ease, but I was still nervous. In the event it was decided that there would be no live witnesses for the committal. Instead the necessary statements would be read to the court and handed in to Mr Peter Badge, Britain's number one magistrate. I was relieved, but it was something of an anti-climax. I had already made plans to take time off work and had lined up somebody to look after my youngest daughter, and I had worked myself up to the point where I just wanted to get it over with.

Instead I stayed at home, wondering what was going on, a terrible fear nagging at my brain: that the magistrate would decide there was no case to answer and Rose would simply walk out through the door. My nightmare, of course, was that her next port of call would be my house. My fear of that woman was still so great I knew that we would have to flee to protect my life and my family.

As it turned out, Carol was ill that week and off school.

As I had already arranged time off work was able to stay at home and look after her. Carol suffers from asthma and often falls foul of infections. That week it was her ears, and the poor little mite felt terrible so I was relieved to be with her. I watched the television reports along with the rest of the country. Because of the legal restrictions no real details were given. The people I knew who attended the hearing — police officers and journalists — were all careful not to reveal anything that was said in the courtroom. Instead they simply called to check that I was all right. Whenever anything official happened in connection with the case the pressure on me seemed to mount and my stress levels rocketed, never more so than at the beginning of May 1995, when Rose appeared at Winchester Crown Court for the pre-trial review. Again, only minimal details were allowed to be made public. But when a television reporter announced that, as expected, Rose had pleaded not guilty to all the charges I felt sick. I suppose I hoped she would have a change of heart and come clean. Then I wouldn't have to give evidence and it would all be over. It was an unrealistic dream, but I couldn't help clinging to it for a while.

Rose was fighting for her own survival. She knew she faced the prospect of spending the rest of her life in prison and she wasn't going to go quietly. It would have been out of character for her to have pleaded guilty just to spare the witnesses the torture of the trial. After all, torture was what it was all about and what she enjoyed most.

That night Phil was away working and I was alone with my worries. I took my tablets and sat watching television but I couldn't concentrate. My mind was spinning and the trial seemed like a dark clouding hanging over me. Would people believe me? Would the defence destroy my reputation to the extent that the jury would think I was simply out for revenge? How could I stand there in front of all those people and describe in intimate detail the horrors I had experienced? How would I deal with the world knowing everything about me and my past? I felt so ashamed of my life. Nothing could convince me it wasn't all my own fault. I might have been a blameless eight-year-old when it all began, but my great fear was that people would see me as I am now, a grown woman, and that they wouldn't understand. While all this was going on I had another big problem. My eldest daughter Michelle, now eleven, was suffering behavioural problems. They were fuelled, I knew, from the constant publicity about her grandfather. After all, what child wouldn't react on discovering that her 'grampy' was a mass murderer? I won't go into great detail about it here because I don't want to add to her difficulties. I hope that one day Michelle will come to terms with our problems and things will be right again. Suffice it to say that the root of my daughter's problem was that she wanted her mother and father back together again. That is understandable; it is very common for children of divorced parents to dream of a reconciliation. But no matter how often I told Michelle that her father and I now led separate lives and it was impossible, she wouldn't give up hope. Consequently she was unhappy about Phil's role and jealous because Carol was able to be with both her parents together. The upshot was that Michelle went to live for a while with her father and his seventeen-year-old girlfriend at the pub he ran in Gloucester. I still saw her every day at school, and I was upset at the change in her. She was smoking and her language was appalling.

I contacted the social services, who monitored Michelle's home life. But I had no power to make her come home. She said that if I insisted she would run away. She would only return if I dumped Phil. I love my daughter, but I couldn't let her run my life. The social services decided that the pub was not a suitable place for Michelle to live, and Chris didn't really want her full-time anyway, and couldn't cope. So she was sent to a foster home. The option to come home was always there, but she chose not to. It hurt like hell, but I had to let my head rule my heart and let her go. I told her I loved her and would always be there, but I wouldn't force her to live with me if she didn't want to.

Michelle's first foster home didn't work out. She wasn't happy there and I wasn't happy about her being there, either. The social services tried their best but I felt I was fighting them all the way. Ideally I wanted my daughter at home, but if that wasn't possible then at least she had to be somewhere where she would be cared for properly and given the help and attention she required. Eventually a more suitable home was found for her and the counselling she so desperately needed was arranged.

While I was worrying myself sick about my eldest daughter and suffering anxiety attacks about the trial, I was dealt yet another blow. I had to give up the one little piece of normality left in my life – my job. It wasn't exactly a career, but I loved working as a dinner lady at the local school both my girls attended. I got on well with the children and had a good relationship with the teachers, the other dinner ladies and the headmistress. The hours fitted in well with taking care of my own children and gave me a break from the constant police interviews. It got me out of the house and gave me something else to think about.

I cannot emphasise enough how important that job was to me. From the moment of my father's arrest I had been living in a twilight world — the curtains in my living room had been pulled tightly shut on that day in February 1994 and stayed that way. It was the only barrier to keep out prying eyes. Of course, I had to go shopping and so on, and as I can't drive I had to catch the bus into town. I didn't look at anyone and tried to not to make eye contact with people in shops. I always felt they knew who I was and would talk about me the minute I was out of hearing range. My fears were often justified, and sometimes they didn't even wait that long. Even in the street where I lived I had problems. Some neighbours were supportive, others gossiped and stared. A group of workmen renovating council houses opposite mine regularly called out insults or fell silent and stared at me whenever I passed. Occasionally they even had the cheek to bang on my door and ask for a cup of tea. They probably just wanted a closer look at Fred West's daughter.

With all this going on I suppose it wasn't surprising that I began to experience trouble at the school. The only astonishing thing was that it took as long as it did to surface. One of the children told another he had seen the ghost of Fred West in the playground. He had yellow eyes and looked like a monster, he said. The story was passed around until some of the younger children became terrified and started asking me if I would turn into a monster too. Fred West was 'out to get them' — would I try to get them too? they asked.

I was devastated. I love children and I was close to many of the youngsters at school. I was proud of the fact that they often turned to me when they hurt themselves in the playground or were unhappy about something. But the Fred West tale got out of hand and became a sort of mass hysteria, causing some of the little ones to sob with fear. Parents complained and I felt I was left with no option but to resign.

The headmistress said she didn't want me to leave and was very supportive, but I just couldn't deal with the look of pure fear on some of the kids' faces when they saw me and I knew it could only get worse. I earned less than £20 a week in that job, but I didn't do it for the money. I did it because I enjoyed it and because it gave me a certain amount of self-respect.

It was hard to come to terms with what happened at school and the experience plunged me once again into a deep depression. I tried to talk to Phil about it and he tried hard to understand, but the whole episode made him angry – not with me but with other people. When he is upset he withdraws into himself and can barely bring himself to talk to me. What I need is reassurance and a cuddle, and he finds that hard.

Once again I did something stupid in my attempt to cope with what life was throwing at me. I took too many of my tablets. They made me feel like I was floating away from my troubles so I took some more. It was Phil who realised I had overdosed. He phoned my GP, who called an ambulance, and I spent another night at Gloucester Hospital. We told Carol and people locally I had dehydrated from the heat. It wasn't a serious attempt to kill myself. Again, I just wanted to blot out my problems for a while. I just didn't know when I was suffering from depression. All of a sudden a big black cloud would settle over me and I felt a wave of despair. Sometimes it cleared and I struggled on; on other occasions it was so tempting just to give in to it. I knew I couldn't, because of the children, but sometimes I simply wasn't capable of thinking straight.

When I came out of hospital that day in July I felt the same way as I had when I ended up in hospital after my father killed himself. I was ashamed of what I had done even though I knew I wasn't in my right mind when I did it. My doctor prescribed valium and once again I tried to get myself back on an even keel and coast through life as the dreaded trial drew nearer and nearer.

When I was barely in my teens and at Cromwell Street I used to have to tidy the younger children's playroom. It was in the cellar — the room we now know my father and Rose used to bury their victims. We had few toys, but my little sisters did have a number of dolls. They would play at dressing them up in different outfits but when it was time for bed they would leave them strewn around the floor, naked with their limbs twisted in different directions.

I used to gently straighten the dolls' arms and legs and dress them in whatever tiny clothes were handy. Then I would lay them all in a line and cover them up with a piece of cloth. I tucked them in as if they were children, stroked their pretty hair and sometimes even kissed them goodnight. I never left them unclothed. I couldn't. It tore at my heart to see them lying there naked and abandoned: I knew how it felt.

I think sometimes of the tortured child I was then and how it comforted me to give my love to those deserted dolls. The innocent affection I heaped on them was what I longed for myself but never received.

I don't suppose I am so different now from that sad youngster who put the dolls to bed. I don't like anyone seeing me undress. I go through all sorts of weird contortions under my huge towel on the beach and change very quickly in shop cubicles when trying on clothes. My sex life is not a matter for discussion here, but it is enough to say that I have been very lucky to find a man as understanding as Phil.

I don't know what other effects the whole experience has had on my life. I suppose my constant need for reassurance that I am a worthwhile person and my desire to compare how other people live with how I live now, must be a one legacy. Obviously I often question my own judgement but I find my need to do what I feel is right is usually a good enough guide. Who knows what will happen when I finally open all the old wounds and confront my past and myself. I only knew I have to do it some time in order to go forward and live a decent life with, and for, my two daughters.

I get similar reactions and questions from every new person I meet – 'You're not what I expected,' or 'How come you seem so normal?' If it is an introduction connected in some way with the police investigation or this book, people are fairly up front, but social occasions are different. Phil and I rarely go out but in the last year we have socialised a little with his family and he has had the job of explaining who I am. Most of his close relatives have been wonderful and welcoming, but people further removed cannot help being curious.

Getting ready for a family party can take me ages. I haven't much choice of what to wear, but I want to get it right and to know that I look OK and will be accepted. Then there is the awful moment when I walk into a room. I glance around and people look away. Then they whisper to each other when they think I'm not looking. 'That's Fred West's daughter. Doesn't she look like him?' At the beginning I wanted to go over to them and say: 'Yes, I am, and yes, I do. But I can't help it and I'm not responsible for what he did.' Now I am more used to it and cope better. I ignore the looks or stare people out. I try to be myself, join in the fun and put people at ease with my sense of humour. I'm naturally quite an easy-going sort of person, but it has been difficult to retain my natural spontaneity over the last two years.

I was very upset at one party when another guest spotted

me chatting to her little daughter and tore across the room to rescue her. She grabbed the child by the hand and dragged her away with a stern exclamation and not a word to me. I love children and they gravitate towards me instinctively, so I was hurt by her action. But at the same time I am a mother, too, and I understand what motivated her, although perhaps she could have been a little bit more diplomatic.

So how is it that most people think I seem so normal? Well, what do they expect? Do they think I will have two heads or walk the streets with an axe in my hand? My father was a serial killer and a rapist. I am not: I am one of his victims, too. I am as normal as anyone can be who has been sexually abused as a child, who has been brought up to believe that her way of life was common, who was forced into prostitution at an age when sex should have been a grown-up word yet to be explained.

These things are inside me but they don't show on the outside, at least, not to strangers. And there aren't many people close to me to know what goes on in my head or my heart. On the surface. I am a passably attractive woman who dyes her hair red to try to disguise her likeness to her father. I try to grow it long for the same reason, even though I prefer it short. When it begins to irritate me I give up and cut it short again, only to stare at my reflection in the mirror and immediately vow to grow it again. With me what you see is what you get. I'm as honest as I can be; I say what I think and what I mean, although I wouldn't deliberately set out to hurt anyone.

Even the social services appear to view me with suspicion. My half-brothers and sisters were taken into care by the local authority when it all began and I haven't been allowed proper contact with them since. I have battled long and hard to keep in touch with them, but the social workers seem to think I am some kind of danger to them, as if I was on trial and not just a witness at someone else's.

I have managed to send birthday and Christmas cards and presents and the occasional message, but one day I want to explain to them why I gave evidence against their mother and why I would have done so against our father; that justice had to be done for the sake of so many people. I hope they won't turn against me and that they won't experience the kind of trauma I have. After all, they, too, will have to live forever with the stigma of being Fred and Rose West's children.

When Stephen and Mae begin to acknowledge what their mum and our father did, I would like to think they too will accept how much I care for them. A family feud between them and me seems to have developed, mainly because I agreed to give evidence at the trial, and, I suppose, because of the newspaper deals and the money that was thrown around when our father was arrested. It didn't take Stephen long to sell his story. I feel I have lost so much of my family; I hope that one day the past can be laid to rest and we can pick up the pieces and get to know each other again.

21

The Trial

As the trial of my stepmother, Rose, approached I began to feel more and more nervous. My family were also finding it difficult and my daughter Carol, just eight years old, was diagnosed as suffering from stress. No matter how hard I tried to make everything seem normal she was sensitive to the atmosphere in the house and viewing every visitor with suspicion. It was impossible to hide the trial from her as the media interest grew once again.

A month before the court case began in Winchester, I came to the boil. I'm sure the police must have thought they had lost their prime witness and I am sorry if I added to their problems but it was inevitable the pressure would get to me. However even at that stage I was determined to make it to the witness stand and do what was right. I never considered backing out but I was anxious to get it over and done with.

I began drinking in the evenings to try and calm my nerves

and build my courage. I couldn't eat or sleep. I was walking an emotional tightrope trying to appear calm and normal for my daughters and friends but constantly re-living the nightmare years in my mind.

One weekend I drank too much and took Phil's car out. Not a wise thing to do considering I don't drive — or at least have never passed a test. What I didn't know was that Phil had slipped a sleeping tablet in my coffee in the hope I would get some rest and relax. For comfort I took along an enormous cuddly toy mouse which Phil had given me once as a present and had strapped him in with a seat belt in the passenger seat.

A frantic and worried Phil called DC Nick Barnes, the officer assigned to look after me, and the local police force was asked to keep an eye out. They found me but not until I had bumped into someone else's car and then into one of their police cars. I know it was a crazy thing to do and don't ask me where I was going because I am not even sure. I just needed to get away from the fear which was beginning to take over my life. Believe me I am not proud of what I did and I am the first to criticise people who drink and drive and risk lives. I'm not offering excuses, just an explanation. The court case was heard about a month later, after I had given evidence at Winchester, and I was banned from driving for 18 months and fined £250.

But the driving incident achieved something. I got attention and reassurance from the right people and it helped me realise I had to calm down and get the job done — for my mother, my sisters, my children and all the others who had suffered. I stopped going walkabout — the phrase Phil and my friends had coined for my occasional disappearance when things got too much — and went on holiday to Norfolk for a week with

Phil and Carol. I returned with my resolve hardened and my mind clear.

For the first day of the court case, I wore a cream coloured angora sweater and a cream skirt. I was determined not to dress in a dark colour and knowing I looked smart gave me confidence. The police picked me up early on the Wednesday morning three weeks into the trial and drove me from my home in Gloucester to Winchester, another attractive city famous for its cathedral. The journey took nearly three hours but I felt relaxed and determined. I knew what I had to do.

As I walked through the witness door into the court room there was an expectant hush. Every eye was on me but I felt quietly confident. I took the oath and gave my name in a clear voice. I looked at the judge, Justice Mantell, in his red robes and dignified wig and asked politely if I might sit down. He gave me a reassuring smile and my courage grew. I smiled back and said thank you and he nodded kindly at me.

As I took my seat, surrounded by microphones, I looked deliberately to my left at my stepmother sitting in the dock. She gave a half smile of acknowledgement and I returned it with a slight nod of my head and a minute movement of my lips. It was the moment I had been dreading. I knew I had to face her and confront my fear and I had done it. From that moment on I knew it would be alright and I would get through the ordeal.

The prosecutor Mr Brian Leveson, QC, a small man with glasses and greying dark hair poking under his wig, asked me a series of questions establishing my identity and place among the West family. I answered each time in a quiet but clear voice knowing I would have to speak up for everyone to hear me in that imposing court room with it's high ceiling and panelled walls. I addressed my answers straight to the jury and any questions I had either to Mr Leveson or the judge.

I was asked about my early life at 25 Midland Road, about my memories of my mother and of Charmaine. As I spoke I played with an engraved gold locket on a chain around my neck. I drew strength and courage from just holding it. It had been given to me by some dear friends the day before I went to Winchester, almost as a good luck charm. In it I had placed a few of the ashes taken from the wooden casket which held the mortal remains of my mother and sister. It may sound a little strange but I felt they were there with me. I was doing this for them and because I knew they would have wanted me to do what was right.

The moment I had been dreading came after about 15 minutes. Mr Leveson dropped his voice, raised his eyes to mine and asked quietly: 'Do you remember your first sexual experience?'

'Yes I do,' I told him.

'How old were you?'

'I was eight.'

'Where was it?'

'It was at 25 Cromwell Street. In the basement, the cellar.'

'Who was involved?'

'My stepmother and my father.'

There was a gasp from the public gallery as I began to tell the judge and jury about what happened to me that day. Mr Leveson let me tell the story in my own words only occasionally interrupting. At one point I said: 'I had my clothes removed.' He asked: 'Do you remember who did that?'

'Rosemary did.'

As I said the words I looked at the woman in the dock.

She sat there dressed in a black jacket and cream blouse nervously moistening her mouth. I looked straight at her and she lowered her head. I carried on with my story. Several times when I said her name or told of what she had done to me I faced her. I faced my fear and she turned away and could not return my gaze.

Despite my growing confidence and the locket I clutched in my hand there were times when it was all too much and I began to cry. I was given a glass of water and took several small sips. I wiped my eyes with a tissue, apologised, and continued to answer the questions and describe some of the most frightening and intimate moments of my life. Mr Leveson and the judge were very gentle and at one point when I was sobbing, my head in my hands, the Judge ordered a ten minute break so I could compose myself.

After the short recess, people in the public gallery craned over to look at me and at Rose. I was asked about the relationship between my father and stepmother, about my sister Heather and more about the abuse I had suffered. I spent most of the day in the witness box and told nothing but the truth. At the end of the afternoon the defence barrister Mr Richard Fergusson, QC, said he was not ready to cross examine me and the judge adjourned. Before doing so he warned me not to talk to anyone about the evidence I had given. Glad that the first part of my ordeal was over and grateful for his kindness throughout I nodded and said quietly 'Thank you my Lord' before leaving the witness box.

It was a huge relief to get through the day I had dreaded so much. But there was more to come. I had to face Mr Richard Fergusson, QC, in cross examination. He would want to question me closely about what I had told the jury. I knew he would suggest I was lying or making it up. It was his job to do so. I was telling the truth but I was still nervous.

I didn't go home after giving evidence the first day. Instead I was put up in an hotel on the South Coast. It was unfortunate that the day after I gave evidence the jury were to go on a planned visit to 25 Cromwell Street. It meant my evidence would be split up and resumed on the Friday morning. The judge had said it was something he wanted to avoid but the timetable had worked out that way.

As it happened it was more than unfortunate. It was too much for me to deal with. I wanted to get it over with and now I was having to wait around for two nights and a day. The fear once again began to build in my mind. I spent the Thursday by the seaside at Bournemouth in the company of a specialist nurse from Gloucester who had been detailed to look after me. She was a nice woman, we got on well and I enjoyed the day.

But in the evening I wanted to be alone and refused all offers from the police for company. I needed space and I felt no one could help me. I spent a substantial amount of the evening drinking and then took some of the drugs the doctor had given me. It was stupid but I wasn't thinking straight. I made a call for help and the police got to me in time. I had my stomach pumped at Southampton Hospital and spent part of the night there.

The next day they could not release me without the permission of a psychiatrist. There wasn't one present and a doctor had to be rushed from Winchester to pass me fit before I could leave the hospital. I was ready and waiting at eight o'clock, determined to finish my evidence. Somehow word had got out and when I left the hospital the press were there. I was late for court and speculation mounted. The judge informed the jury only that I had been 'indisposed' over night and ordered the press not to release why for the duration of the trial.

Dressed in a burgundy and cream blouse and a burgundy skirt I took the stand once again. I was questioned by Mr Fergusson about Heather, about the victim Shirley Robinson, who had lived with the family, and about my teenage years and sexual experiences with my father. Then, in his broad Belfast accent, he said: 'I suggest to you that your stepmother never bound or gagged you.'

I replied, 'Yes, my stepmother did.'

'I suggest to you that she never sexually abused you or was present when you were.'

'Yes, my stepmother was.'

He suggested this incident I had described in the cellar never took place. Quietly I replied: 'The things that I have said in court have been the truth.'

When it was over the sense of relief was enormous. I was ecstatic, I had got through it, done what was right and proved to myself and everybody else that I could. I had faced my fear and lived through it. Of course later that weekend I came crashing down. The trial wasn't over, my life was the same and there were still problems ahead, but nevertheless the feeling of having done the right thing, and knowing my mum would be proud of me, remained.

22

The Verdict

GUILTY – the word rang out around the sombre courtroom at Winchester. The foreman of the jury looked at the judge as he delivered the verdict. Mr Justice Mantell thanked the men and women who had spent seven weeks deliberating the future of my stepmother and turned towards the desk where she sat. The rest is a blur. Those tense moments as the jury filed back in had left me trembling. The sense of anticipation as they took their seats before announcing their findings was electric. All around me sat the families of other victims struggling with their emotions.

Someone let out a cry, someone else murmured 'Thank God', and several people wiped tears from their eyes. I just sat there. I was glad I had been vindicated. That people had accepted the truth of what I had said in the witness box. I felt glad for the families of the victims who must have felt they had justice at last. But I was overwhelmed too by a sense of grief. I had helped send my stepmother to prison and sentenced my young half-brothers and sisters to a life without their mother.

I was numb. I couldn't have stood up, my legs would not have held me. But somewhere in those confused emotions was a feeling of relief that it was over. I had done my duty and come through it. There was still my father's inquest to deal with and my sister Heather's funeral to attend. But the major part of my ordeal was finished and maybe now I could start thinking about putting my life in order.

I wanted my family. I wanted to hold my girls tight and never let them go. And I wanted to tell Phil how much he meant to me and how I could not have made it without him. We were sitting separately in the public gallery. Phil and I had made a decision early on that although I had been thrust into the public eye by an accident of birth, he should try to remain anonymous.

The last eighteen months or so had turned my life upside down. I was public property. I had appeared in the witness box and told the world about my bizarre upbringing, my suffering, and the life I had been forced to lead. People would stare at me when I was in town shopping or taking my daughters for a day out. There had to be someone in the family who could carry on and make life appear normal for my two girls, so that at least one of us could leave the house without attracting attention. So Phil has stayed in the background, supportive, kind, good natured, clinging on to a sense of humour which has helped us all to keep going, and, above all, always being there.

We never really made plans for the future, there was too much going on. Sometimes in my mind I wasn't even sure if there *was* a future; I just couldn't see an end to it all. In some ways there never will be. I know in years to come there will be more Fred and Rose West stories in the Press, they will take over from the Brady and Hindley headlines which have never ceased to fascinate the public. I can't argue with that.

I want to disappear, start a new life, but I know its not possible. No matter where I go someone will find me or recognise me. I look too much like my dad to hide forever. In any case I am not sure I want to, I don't want me and my girls to be punished anymore for what my father and Rose did. I want to be able to hold my head up and know I did the right thing. Now that the trial is over I'm getting help. The counsellor told me it would take a lot of hard work and there is a long road ahead – but it is one I want to travel.

Phil and I will leave Gloucester, a new environment will be better for the children and I don't think it would be right for us to stay. A friend told me I should work with children who have been abused like me. He said: "Children would know you could help them. You're a great listener and you would understand them so much better than a social worker who has no experience of what they have been through."

It is a thought. I've always wanted to have enough money to buy a huge house and fill it with children who have suffered. In my dreams I have showered them with the love and affection that I never had and helped them to overcome their problems and go on to lead happy and fulfilled lives.

Speaking out about what happened to me might already have helped other children. No one knew or seemed to care what went on behind the iron gates of 25 Cromwell Street; perhaps now people will look more carefully and spot the danger signs in time. But I have to help myself and my own family first and then maybe I can be of some use to others.

Sometimes when I am sitting with Phil watching my

daughters play I feel a tremendous sense of optimism, because I know I am doing all I can to give them a normal childhood and a good life.

I have lived all my life in the shadows. Now I have been forced into the spotlight and some people will criticize me for the way I have handled it, but I'm doing the best I can. And as the shadows fade I can see a light at the end of the tunnel and I will reach it.

On Wednesday 22 November 1995 Rosemary Pauline West was sentenced to life for the murders of 10 young women and girls, including Heather West and Charmaine West. The Judge, Mr Justice Mantell, QC, said 'If attention is paid to what I think you will never be released. Take her down.'

The Victims

Catherine Costello, Anna-Marie West's mother, was born in Glasgow on 14 April 1944, one of five daughters. She left her home in Scotland to stay with a friend in the village of Much Marcle. There she met Fred West, and married him on 17 November 1962.

When she vanished, some time between March and December of 1970, the couple were separated and Catherine, or Rena as she was known, was living at the Watermead Caravan Park at Brockworth in Gloucester. She was never reported missing to the police. Her family thought she had run away with another man and was living abroad somewhere, a story put about by Fred.

Her body was found at 10.30 a.m. on 11 April 1994 in Letterbox Field, Much Marcle. Bones were scooped up by a mechanical digger which was excavating the site as part of the police search. A right thigh bone, shin and fibula plus footbones were discovered first. Then the left thigh bone and other remains were uncovered about two feet below the surface in thick, reddish clay. The jawbone, the base of the skull and teeth were also present. Bit by bit, the police sifted through the soil until they discovered the entire skeleton of a woman of about 5ft 3ins tall.

A dental examination revealed that the woman was aged between twenty-three and thirty when she died. There were no dental records available for Catherine Costello, but using photo and video technology to recreate an image from the skull, it was later concluded that the remains were indeed hers.

Charmaine West was born on 22 March 1963 in Lanarkshire, Scotland. Her mother was Catherine Costello; her father is believed to have been an Asian man living in Glasgow.

The following year Catherine had another child, Anna-Marie, by Fred West, to whom she was by this time married. The four of them lived together as a family until Fred and Rena split up in 1965. Charmaine and her sister were in and out of the care of the social services for some years before settling at Midland Road, Gloucester with Fred and his new girlfriend, Rose.

Charmaine was last seen around March 1971. Thereafter relatives, neighbours and the authorities were told she had gone to live with her natural mother, but there was no trace of either of them.

When Rose West was first questioned by police about Charmaine – in 1992, during the investigation into an assault on another child in the family – she still maintained that the child had been taken by Catherine Costello. Quizzed later, in February 1994, before the body was found, she again insisted that Charmaine had been collected from Midland Road by her mother around March 1971. It is now known that by then Catherine Costello was already dead.

On 4 March 1994, a warrant was obtained to search the premises at 25 Midland Road. The search began on 25 April. It was ten days before Charmaine's body was found on 4 May.

It was discovered under a newly built kitchen extension at a depth of 2.19m.

The child had been placed in a foetal position, on her back with her spine curved forward and her arms outstretched. Professor Bernard Knight, who examined the body in situ, said that her legs might have been amputated at hip level, or the remains may might been disturbed by building work. Pieces of coal around the body indicated that she had been killed and hidden elsewhere first, possibly in a coal shed or bunker, and buried later.

Heather West, the daughter of Fred and Rose West, was born on 17 October 1970 in Gloucester. She was the couple's first child, arriving when Anna-Marie was six and Rose was still a teenager and not yet married to Fred.

Heather vanished in the summer of 1987. She had just finished secondary school and was nearly seventeen. Her parents reported sightings of her and telephone calls from her, but she was never seen by anyone else after the day she allegedly left home following a row.

Heather's body was found buried under the patio of 25 Cromwell Street, the family home where she grew up and spent most of her life, on 26 February 1994. The discovery sparked the Cromwell Street investigation which resulted in the Wests being charged with multiple murder. The remains were located by police digging in the back garden of the Wests' home. They were disordered, with arms, legs, trunk and skull at different levels.

Heather had been decapitated and the body was dismembered at the hips. The job had been done using chopping-type blows with some kind of heavy implement. Black plastic bin liners were found around the trunk and a considerable amount of dark brown hair was with the skull, according to Home Office pathologist Bernard Knight. Part of a necklace was also discovered with the body along with several detached fingernails.

Anne McFall was born in Scotland on 8 April 1949. She was a friend of Catherine Costello and was taken on by the West family to look after Charmaine and Anna-Marie. Fred began an affair with the young nanny. When she died she was eighteen years old and about six months' pregnant.

Anne's last known address was the Timberland Caravan Park, Brockworth, Gloucester, where she was living with Fred and the two children, when they were not in care. She was last seen in May 1967. Her family made considerable efforts to find her, without success.

Anne McFall's remains were found on the evening of 7 June 1994 in Fingerpost Field, Much Marcle. The police were convinced there was a body there and had excavated a site the size of a swimming pool. Close to the wooded area of the field the diggers eventually found bones and a skull. The skull was split in two parts but there was no way of knowing whether it had been buried like that or if the excavation work had caused the damage. The body had been placed in a roughly rectangular pit dug in the day and covered with loose topsoil. It was lying face down in the soil and the facial bones were virtually intact. Scene-of-crimes officers sifting through the soil unearthed the entire skeleton in continuity. The spinal column was laid out in a line, suggesting that the body had not been dismembered like many of those retrieved from the cellar of 25 Cromwell Street.

Scattered near the pelvic area of the body were bones from a foetus described by the pathologist as those of an immature infant. The baby had still been inside its mother when she died. Later it was decided that the pregnancy had been in its sixth or possibly seventh month.

Examination of the remains revealed them to be those of a woman 5ft 2ins tall, aged between seventeen and twenty-three, who had a very high, smooth forehead. The body was identified as that of Anne McFall. Old photographs were compared with the computer reconstruction from the skull to confirm this.

The police had to break the news to her brother in Scotland, who had never given up hope that she was alive.

Lynda Gough was born in Gloucester on 1 May 1953, the eldest of three children. She had a conventional childhood and in 1969, at the age of sixteen, she left school to start work as seamstress at the Co-op in Gloucester. Lynda's family say that about 1972, when she was nineteen, she became more independent, although she continued to live at home with them. She was already visiting 25 Cromwell Street on a regular basis. There were several male lodgers living on the upper floors and she was having a sexual relationship with two of them. Both men confirmed this to police years later. One said that Lynda occasionally looked after Rose West's children.

Some time in March or April 1973, Lynda told her parents that she had found herself a flat in Cromwell Street and would be moving out. A week later a man and a woman called at her family home to take her out for a drink. They said they lived in Cromwell Street. Mrs Gough described the man as Spanish-looking with dark hair and a sallow complexion.

Lynda went with the couple. Her mother believed that the woman played a prominent part in persuading her daughter to leave home. On 19 April 1973, the Goughs all went to work as usual. When Mr Gough returned home at lunchtime he discovered that Lynda had removed all her possessions. She had left a short handwritten note: 'Dear Mum and Dad, please don't worry about me. I've got a flat. I'll come and see you some time. Love, Lynda.'

It was the last contact the Goughs were to have with their daughter.

Mr and Mrs Gough grew worried about Lynda and her mother began to make her own inquiries, which led, about ten days later, to 25 Cromwell Street.

A man and a woman came to the door. The woman was the one who had called for Lynda some weeks earlier. Mrs Gough told her she had come to see Lynda. At first the couple denied that Lynda had ever been at the house, but when Mrs Gough pointed out that the woman was wearing her daughter slippers and that some of her clothes were hanging on the washing line, they changed their story. The woman, Rose West, told Mrs Gough that Lynda had been at the house but had left, possibly heading for Weston-super-Mare. She was not clear on details.

Other tenants at the house had been told by the Wests that Lynda had been babysitting Anna-Marie and had hit her. Fred and Rose claimed they had told the young woman to clear off and she had left.

Mrs Gough contacted the DHSS and the Salvation Army but no one had any news of her daughter. It was to be another twenty-one years before she discovered the truth.

Lynda's remains were found on 7 March 1994 beneath the bathroom of 25 Cromwell Street, which had previously been a garage. She had been dumped in what had once been the inspection pit, which had been filled in with earth, metal and other debris.

A ring mask of adhesive tape was found close to the skull. There were two long pieces of tape, a long piece of string and fragments of dark, knotted fabric. There were many fine cut marks near the upper thigh bones, suggesting disarticulation of the hip joints and dismemberment of the body. The skull was found separately. A number of vertebrae were missing and the body had probably been decapitated.

A dental expert put the age of the victim at nineteen plus, Lynda's age when she vanished.

The ring mask was examined by forensic scientists, who said that a piece of 2in-wide brown tape had been wound in a circle in an overlapping fashion with white tape and some 1½in-wide surgical tape. The ring mask was 15ins in circumference. Small tubes found by the body were also examined. The experts formed the opinion that the tape was used to gag the victim and bind up the head. The tubes were then inserted so that she could breathe. The prosecution contended that the purpose of the tape was to keep Lynda alive but silent, and was a clear indication of sexual abuse before death.

Lynda died in April 1973, four months after another young woman, Caroline Owens, had reported the Wests to the police for kidnap and rape. The Wests had been fined for assault.

Carol Ann Cooper was born on 10 April 1958. Her parents separated in 1962, and Carol stayed with her mother, who died in 1966. For the next two years she lived with her father, who had returned to the area and remarried. The arrangement was not successful, and in 1971 Carol was taken into care and placed at The Pines children's home in Worcester. She became known as Caz, had a tattoo on her forearm and was troublesome, absconding for days at a stretch.

In November 1973 she went missing again but this time she did not return. She was reported as a missing person, but local publicity and TV appeals yielded nothing.

The police believe that Carol was probably hitch-hiking when she was picked up by Fred and Rose West and taken to Cromwell Street. Her remains were found in the cellar of their home.

Her skeleton was excavated from a depth of about 3ft. The bones were layered, with the skull at the bottom. Around the skull was an elasticated cloth band 3ins wide and up to 7ins in diameter. It was wrapped around the lower part of the skull, covering the jaw, lower face and back of the head. A loop of fabric with a half-hitch knot was tied under the forearms. There was a clothesline rope nearby. Also present was a headband of surgical tape wound around itself several times and there were several hair samples on the inside of the tape. The band covered the lower part of the face as gag.

Professor Knight estimated the age of the skeletal remains to be between fifteen and seventeen years. The upper end of the thigh bone showed fine cut marks, there was a gouge in the left femur and the hip joints had been severed with a sharp blade. There were also cuts on the neck and evidence of decapitation. The bones were jumbled in a random way which suggested dismemberment.

A dental examination of the skull put the victim between fifteen and a half and nineteen years of age. Carol was fifteen and a half when she disappeared.

Lucy Partington was born on 4 March 1952 and attended a girls' grammar school in Cheltenham. She left there at the end of the summer term in 1971 and in the autumn went to Exeter University to study medieval English.

During the Michaelmas term of 1973 Lucy, a committed Christian, was received into the Catholic Church. On 20 December she returned home to Gretton, a village near Cheltenham, to spend Christmas with her family. She left the house on 27 December to visit a disabled friend, Helen Render, who lived in the centre of Cheltenham, just off the A435, the Cheltenham to Evesham trunk road. Lucy and Helen, who was confined to a wheelchair, had been friends for four years. Lucy had already visited her several times over the holiday and that night they sat down and discussed their shared interest in medieval English. Helen helped Lucy to write a letter to the Courtauld Institute, where she hoped to study for an MA in medieval art. Lucy left at about 10 p.m., taking the letter with her, and rushed to catch her last bus home. The bus stop was about a three-minute walk from Helen's home. If she missed the connection she always returned to her friend's house, knowing that Helen's father would give her a lift. But that night she did not return and was never seen again.

Extensive police inquiries were made at the time but there were no sightings of Lucy. The prosecution argued that 'this gentle, serious, chaste girl must have been picked up at the bus stop'.

The police eventually found Lucy more than twenty years later, on 6 March 1994. She was buried 2ft 6ins down in the basement of 25 Cromwell Street. Her body was discovered in what was known as the 'nursery corner' of the cellar, where the wallpaper was decorated with cartoon and nursery characters. In later years the Wests had let their young children sleep there.

Professor Knight's examination found the skull upside down. Two pieces of woven cord, 1/4in thick, were knotted together below the jaw. A knife was also found alongside the remains. It was made of stainless steel, honed down and still sharp. There were three cut marks on the right femur and also on the left, sharp edges around the hip joints and signs of decapitation. Dental examination put the age of the victim at twenty plus. Lucy was twenty-one when she vanished.

Records held at Gloucester Royal Hospital showed that Fred West had been treated there for a laceration to his right hand at 12.25 a.m. on 3 January 1974, seven days after Lucy went missing. The police believe Fred injured himself while dismembering the body. Their conclusion was that Lucy had been kept bound and gagged in the cellar at Cromwell Street before being killed. They said that Lucy would have been extremely reluctant to accept a lift from a stranger but may have been reassured by the presence of a woman in the car.

Therese Siegenthaler was born on 27 November 1952 in Switzerland. In 1974 she was living in Deptford, South London and studying sociology at Woolwich Polytechnic. She was a quiet but confident girl, and able to take care of herself. She looked young for her age, wore no make-up and spoke fluent English with a Swiss–German accent.

At Easter 1974 Therese planned to travel to Roscannon in Ireland to meet a priest she knew who shared her interest in South Africa. She planned to be away for one week and had arranged to go to the theatre with another friend on her return. She had already bought the theatre ticket.

Therese decided to hitch-hike from London to Holyhead and catch a ferry across the Irish Sea. On the evening of 15 April she went to a party at a friend's house in north London

Out of the Shadows

and the next day she set off, carrying a small backpack containing her Swiss passport and enough money for the ferry and to live on for a week in Ireland. She was never seen again.

Therese was due back in London on 23 April. When she hadn't arrived by the following day, her friend notified the police. Extensive inquiries were made but no trace of the student was found.

On 5 March 1994, almost twenty years later, Therese's remains were unearthed in the cellar of 25 Cromwell Street. She had no connection with Gloucester, the Wests or Cromwell Street. The police believe she was another random victim picked up by Fred and Rose while hitch-hiking.

Therese's body was found compressed in a 2ft by 3ft area in front of an imitation fireplace in the cellar. Professor Knight said that the remains were in anatomical disarray, with the limbs on top of the trunk and head. One arm was above the skull, which was lying face down. In the grave with her was a knotted cloth loop made of something similar to stocking material, which had presumably slipped off the skull. There were numerous small injuries to the bones, with fine cuts to the left thigh bone, and multiple cuts to the vertebrae which pointed to decapitation. Forensic experts found threads of pink cloth, which could have been part of her clothing, and a hair decoration. Also discovered near the body was a square silk scarf, folded or rolled to form a loop. Fragments of brown hair were trapped inside the knotted part of the material.

Dental examination put the victim's age at twenty plus. Therese was twenty-one.

Shirley Hubbard was the victim about whom least was known but whose remains were the first to reveal the most chilling aspects of all. Shirley, the daughter of Glynis Lloyd and Owen John Owen, was born in Birmingham on 26 June 1954. Later her parents moved to Worcester. They separated when she was about two years old and she was taken into care. At the age of six she was placed with foster parents named Hubbard in Droitwich.

In October 1974, Shirley, described as very pretty and young-looking, ran away from home, leaving a note for her parents. They contacted the police, who found her camping in a field near Worcester. A few weeks later, on 15 November 1974, she disappeared again. She had left home that morning to go to Debenhams department store in Worcester, where she was doing work experience. She had no possessions with her. Shirley never returned, and Mrs Hubbard never heard from her or of her again. The police and social services tried to find the child but came up with nothing.

Shirley's remains were unearthed at Cromwell Street on 5 March 1994 in a part of the basement decorated with pictures of Marilyn Monroe. The police said she had been subjected to a truly dreadful ordeal. They had to dig through concrete to retrieve her. She had been decapitated and her legs were separate from the rest of the body. Professor Knight also found some significant evidence, which was present again two days later with the discovery of Lynda Gough, when he examined the skull.

It was totally encased in a mask made from windings of brown tape from below chin to eye level. Inserted into the front of the mask was a narrow plastic tube at nostril level. There were three inches of tubing inside which would have entered the nostril. Also found with the body was a second length of tubing.

Forensic experts later confirmed that a length of pale grey

or brown tape had been wrapped round the skull in an overlapping manner from the chin to the top of the skull. They found hair fragments inside the mask. The police believed that the tubing was significant because it showed that the victim had been alive when the mask was applied. It had been used to keep her living and breathing throughout whatever cruelty it was that she experienced at the hands of the Wests.

Prosecuting barrister Neil Butterfield QC told Rose West's committal hearing:

> She would have been at the mercy of whoever did this to her. She was kept alive and helpless for sexual gratification so her living and restrained body could be used or abused at will. How long she survived, how long she was abused, and how ultimately she died we cannot say. But it is proper to infer that such abuse took place at Cromwell Street: it would have been difficult to apply that dreadful mask without the assistance of more than one person.

Juanita Mott, the middle child of three sisters, was born on 1 March 1957. The family lived in Colney Hill, Gloucester. Juanita was a rebellious and self-willed child, and when her parents split up and her mother remarried, her family life became unsettled. She left school when she was fifteen years old. In the summer of 1974 she met a young man called Timothy Davis. Juanita was then living in a flat in Stroud Road, Gloucester, but a few weeks after meeting Timothy she moved to 25 Cromwell Street. Timothy never went beyond the doorstep of the house but on several occasions he called for Juanita there.

The teenager was very friendly with a woman called Jennifer Baldwin, an old friend of her mother's with whom she had stayed for a few months when she first left home. Some time at the beginning of 1975, Juanita left Cromwell Street and moved back in with Mrs Baldwin. Mrs Baldwin was due to get remarry on 12 April, and it was arranged that Juanita, by now eighteen, would look after her young children that day.

The night before the wedding Juanita went out for the evening. She was in the habit of thumbing a lift into Gloucester from Mrs Baldwin's home in Newent. She did not come home that night, neither did she turn up as promised the following day to take care of the children. She was never seen again.

On 6 March 1994 Juanita's remains were found in the basement at Cromwell Street. The pathologist reported that the bones were in disarray and a clothesline-type rope was wound around the body. There were two small wrist-sized loops in the rope. Around the skull was a a band of fabric, running around the jaw to the top of the head and round the back of it. It was formed from a continuous length of material made from bits of clothing knotted together to form a makeshift mask.

There were signs that the body had been cut up at the hips and decapitated. At the top of the skull was a depressed fracture where the bone was cracked and crushed inwards. Professor Knight said that this could have been caused by a heavy blow from a circular object similar to a ball-headed hammer, but he stressed that the fracture could have been inflicted after decapitation.

The forensic experts who examined the ropes and mask found in the grave with Juanita described them as two pieces of grey plastic cord similar to washing line, one measuring 10ft and the other 7ft. The ropes contained a series of loops made with slip knots and one had a piece of ribbon tied to it. The mask was made from two long nylon socks, a bra and a pair of tights knotted together.

Prosecutor Neil Butterfield said after outlining Juanita's story: 'The cellar at 25 Cromwell Street was now full of bodies, five of them buried in it. It was at that point in 1975 or 1976 that the floor was concreted over and the area used as bedroom accommodation for the children.'

Shirley Robinson was born on 8 October 1959 in Rutland, where her parents lived at RAF Cottesmore. In 1962 they split up and initially Shirley stayed with her mother, her father taking her on the following year because of domestic difficulties. In 1974, aged nearly fifteen, she went back to her mother, who was living in Hartlepool, but things didn't work out. She was placed in the care of Bristol Social Services and her mother lost touch with her.

Shirley was sent to the Crescent School, Downend, Bristol and was originally housed in a secure unit. By 1975 she had been transferred to the cottages used to accommodate the girls who had started work. A residential social worker there recalled her concern about Shirley, whom she thought was beginning to show lesbian tendencies. The teenager had a factory job for a short time and in 1977 responsibility for her supervision was transferred to Gloucester Social Services. Shirley then got a live-in job as a housemaid at Chipping Sodbury.

The next trace police found of her movements was when she registered with a Gloucester surgery as a patient on 21 June 1977, giving her address as 25 Cromwell Street. By that autumn she was pregnant – there are records of a positive test on 18 October. She did not name the child's father, but it was generally assumed to be Fred West.

Another lodger at Cromwell Street, Liz Brewer, told the police that when she moved there in April 1977 Shirley was already there. Rose West was also pregnant at about the same time and gave birth in December 1977 to a half-caste child. Liz said it was common knowledge that Shirley was having Fred's baby. Rose West told the same story to other neighbours, and although at first she seemed to accept the situation, she became increasingly jealous as Shirley flaunted her developing pregnancy. There is evidence too that Rose was attracted to Shirley and at one time had a lesbian affair with her.

Liz Brewer noticed the growing tension in the household. Shirley, she said, became more and more emotional, declaring her love for Fred. There were frequent rows and Shirley asked if she could stay in Liz's room at the top of the house.

The last day anyone saw Shirley was 9 May 1978. By this time she was eight months' pregnant. She and Liz had gone to Woolworths in Gloucester and had had their pictures taken in a booth. Liz wrote the date on the back. The following day Liz went out, leaving Shirley behind in her bedsit. She returned later to find that she had gone. Liz's first thought was that she had made it up with Fred and Rose and gone back to her old room. But she hadn't. She had apparently vanished off the face of the earth, and Liz never saw her again.

Another lodger, Claire Rigby, who occupied the room opposite Shirley's, saw Rose West clearing out Shirley's belongings and packing them into plastic bags. It was obvious she had taken nothing with her. When an official from the

DHSS came to check up on Shirley nearly three months later, Rose told him that she had gone to Germany leaving no forwarding address.

On 28 February 1994 the remains of Shirley Robinson and her unborn child were uncovered in the rear garden of Cromwell Street. One bone was poking up through the soil.

Shirley's body was one of only two found without any accompanying restraining materials, the other being that of Heather West. There were deep chop marks on the body which had severed the bones completely. Professor Knight said that they had probably been made with a very sharp blade such as that of a cleaver or heavy knife. There were twenty-one fine cuts slicing the fifth cervical vertebra, which indicated that she had been decapitated.

The prosecution contended that Shirley had been murdered because she threatened the stability of the relationship between Fred and Rose West.

Alison Chambers was born on 8 September 1962 in Swansea. After her parents split up in the early 1970s she became something of a rebellious teenager. In 1977 she was taken into care by Swansea Social Services and placed in a local children's home, from which she ran away on a number of occasions.

At the beginning of January 1979 she was transferred to Jordansbrook Children's Home in Gloucester, from which she also absconded several times. While she was living there Alison started work experience at a local solicitor's office as an office junior. She became friendly with another Jordansbrook girl, Sharon Compton, and the two of them became frequent visitors to 25 Cromwell Street, where they had another friend called Sandra. It was through Sandra that they met Rose West.

Rose began to take an interest in Alison, who told her that she was unhappy at the children's home. Rose described to the young girl an idyllic farm which she claimed she and Fred owned. She told Alison that when she was seventeen she could leave the children's home and go and live on the farm. She talked of walking in the fields and riding horses, and even showed her photographs, which came from an estate agent's details. Alison's friends say she became obsessed with the idea of going to live at the farm in these pictures and talked of nothing else.

Another Cromwell Street lodger at the time, Gillian Brill, remembers a girl called Ali who visited the house regularly. She noted that the girl had lesbian tendencies. That September Alison turned seventeen, and her mother, who had not seen her since January, received a long letter from her. In it Alison said she was living with a very homely family, looking after their five children and doing some housework. The letter was postmarked Northamptonshire. The police believe that Alison had asked a friend to post it from there.

One day Alison failed to turn up for her work experience job. At about the same time she went back to the children's home to collect some belongings, which she put into a rucksack. She was due to return the following day to meet a friend and collect some more of her things, but she didn't come. She was never seen again.

Alison's body was dug up from the garden at Cromwell Street on 28 February 1994. It was under the patio, which had been built soon after she disappeared.

Professor Knight said that the bones were mixed up. The skull was lying sideways and had a white plastic or leather buckled belt fastened around it. There were hair fragments still attached. Unlike the other bodies, there were no obvious injuries to the bones, but the pathologist concluded that the body had still been divided into sections before burial.

Neil Butterfield QC said that Alison had been 'enticed into a sexual relationship with Rose West with false promises of a wonderful, carefree and happy life at a farm. But it was all lies.' He said the belt was put around her face to stop her screaming. 'Why should she want to scream?' he asked. 'Because she was being abused.'

For my son

Daniel,

a coach whose intuitive understanding of sports from an early age reminds me of Peahead Walker.

I was thinking of Dan and sports and history and books when this idea popped into my head.

I thought of him often as I was writing it.

Hopefully he'll enjoy it, and not pick up too much of Coach Walker's vocabulary.